Animal Antics 2008

forwardpress

Edited by Aimée Vanstone
& Donna Samworth

First published in Great Britain in 2008 by:
Forward Press Ltd
Remus House
Coltsfoot Drive
Peterborough
PE2 9JX
Telephone: 01733 898108
Website: www.forwardpress.co.uk

SB ISBN 978-1-84418-472-9

Foreword

To all the authors and contributors, thank you once again for your many (and varied) entries for our Animal Antics 2008 collection! It was, as always, a phenomenal and magical task to sort through the many dedications to the creatures we hold dearest. This journey through the antics of closest companions is the result of much hard work by all involved.

Contained within these pages is an array of poetry that opens up a whole new world of adoration, admiration and understanding whether or not you have your own pets. There are also the authors' favourite pictures of their dogs, cats, rabbits, hamsters, reptiles(!), pigs and many more visions of mayhem, loyalty and devotion.

Animal Antics 2008 is the result of all the authors' hard work and we at Forward Press hope you enjoy the photographs, laughter and reminiscences as much as we have.

Contents

The Poems

To Benjamin - A Bullmastiff

'Benjamin!'
Say his name and he will come.

Fetch him from his deepest sleep,
From all his animal desires,
From all his wild, instinctive ways,
Say his name and he is there!

Though just a puppy he would come,
Small and square and self-contained,
Yet would he frown and trot to see
If Benjamin were he!
Though just a puppy he would come,
But that was curiosity
Because his unexploited heart
Had not then learnt to love.

Though all his past is untamed, free,
From earliest beginnings,
Now all of this has ceased to be
See in his eyes, his soul shines through,
One great, unquestioning love for you.

He lies before the dying fire,
That still gleams amber in his eyes,
As in his rough, rumbustious days
When his great strength
Was yours to prize.

His heavy, sculptured head is low,
His questing muzzle still.
Uncomprehending mists
Dull the agile canine mind.
You cannot long be with him now,
You cannot tell him why.
You cannot tell him how you feel
Now that he soon must die.
Ben, Ben, Benny, Benjamin,
Though death calls loudly all around,
Speak his name; your call is louder,
A spark still kindles at the sound.
Call him for he always comes,

Call him from eternity,
Call him, never let him go,
What canine Heaven can he know
When all his life is you and you are here, below?

Benjamin,
Say his name and he will come.
Your voice, his name,
Are all he knows,
And all he's wished to know.

Molly Mettam

Congratulations Molly!

To Benjamin - A Bullmastiff **has been chosen as the winning poem in this collection by our panel of editors. Your poem has won you our first prize of £1000!**

Nipper

Well, hello chums, my name is Nipper,
And I'm pictured here chewing my slipper.
I'm just a young pup as you can see,
And there is no craftier Jack Russell than me.
When my owners are out, I have a good chew,
Rugs, skirting boards and a chair leg or two!
I even pinch chocolates off the Christmas tree
Although the wrappers are a bit too chewy for me.
It's funny how people rush to the loo,
I tiddle on the floor cos it's what pups do
And if my owners are washing and combing their hair,
I run outside with their underwear.
I love my new home, it's really nice,
Although I've been ticked off once or twice.
I once pulled the edge of the tablecloth
And crashing to the floor came a bowl of broth!
Still, they always forgive little old me,
Cos I suppose they really love me you see.
They even let me sleep on their bed at night,
I know I'm spoilt, but at least I sleep tight.
And in the morning, I have a jolly good feed
And drop at their feet my brand new lead.
Then if they dare to sit down for a talk,
I'll yap and yap till I get my walk.
So as you can see I'm a crafty little soul,
I'm a pup who likes to be in control.
But I'm a happy and contented little Nipper,
So goodbye chums, now, where's my slipper?

Lesley Collins

Taking The Biscuit

It's very nearly dinner time and Jacob's jumping up
I get up from my chair and say, 'Come on then pup.'
He's telling me he's hungry and it's time he had his meal,
So I go into the kitchen and he follows me at heel.

He watches me with interest as I prepare his tin of Chum,
Original, rabbit, beef and heart, he'll eat them as they come.
He doesn't mind the flavour; he just likes his plate of meat,
Occasionally there's rice or pasta with it as a treat.

Then when his meat is finished, he'll back off from his dish,
Licking at his whiskers and looking slightly tigerish.
He looks round for his biscuits; he's got six ovals on the mat,
But he asks for a marrowbone Markie, and then trots off with that.

He usually takes it to the lounge and eats it up in one,
He takes no interest in the ovals until TV is on.
All six biscuits lie there, abandoned on the floor,
Until animals come on TV, that's what he's waiting for.

He doesn't care about the news, or any quiz that's on,
But let anything with cats appear or Wildlife on One.
In fact, if any animal's on screen, then Jacob's on the prowl,
He takes his biscuits one by one and eats them with a growl!

Then he'll rescue his last biscuit from the TV cat,
And bury it securely under the sheepskin mat.
And so that no one else but he his treasure can expose,
He'll push it deep beneath the rug, with long sweeps of his nose.

He knows he shouldn't be hiding his biscuits under the mat,
But he'll do anything at all to keep them from that cat!
He knows, too that I won't like it, and looks innocent as a lamb
When he turns round to see if I'm watching him - I am!

E J Earley

Family Friend

I sigh in grief; I feel a dull pain,
My four-legged friend will return never again,
In peace he sleeps, in rest he lies,
No more shall I see those big brown eyes.

Never to comb his long shaggy hair,
Or shoo him off my favourite chair,
See him bark at the local cat,
Sound asleep on the fireside mat.

Sitting and playing with his collar and lead,
Remembering those evenings when he'd almost plead
And thinking to myself, if he could talk,
He'd ask to be taken for his nightly walk.

We'd stroll for miles and if he could,
He'd slip his lead and run into the wood,
Then chase a squirrel to branch on high,
Then by the tree bowl he'd sit and cry.

His favourite haunt was pond or stream,
To swim and splash and it would seem
Come out of the water and give a shake
Deliberately catching me in water's wake.

The times I've shouted and slapped his hide,
Then felt so mean and tried to hide,
My shame at giving this friend a maul
When just a word would have settled it all.

And I happily recall, oft' times, he'd be wrapped
In shawl and blanket cos he'd been trapped
By grandchildren, to play, a baby in arms
And not even whimper or have any qualms.

We'd had him so long, from a puppy in fact,
A member of the family, he deserved at least that,
So to lose him was a bombshell. Why did he have to go?
None of us will forget him, we all miss him so.

W G Stannard

My Big Izzy

He's two years old and big and fluffy
he thinks he's a really big toughie.
All that fluff is usually very frizzy
but he's soft and silly is my big Izzy.

He eats and sleeps and is misunderstood
at night he goes prowling the neighbourhood.
He charges the cat flap like a bull at a gate
when I call 'tuna' he thinks he'll be late.

Izzy likes to snuggle and pad with his paws
he twitches in his sleep and even snores.
Around in circles he chases the torch
not sure what is in his thoughts.

He can be a real big bully to his sister Roo
but he then gets a telling off and a talking too!
He shakes his tail and saunters over
and starts to purr just like Casanova.

In someone else's bed is where you will find Izzy
you can be sure he's sleeping, he's never busy.
At meal time he's there well before you
but we love big Izzy, yes we do.

Angela Boswell

If Rosie Were A Person...

If Rosie were a person, she'd be your favourite nan.
Bit forgetful, always pleased to see you,
And a friendly face to welcome you home.

She'd be one of those kind people who always give to charity
For no reason, other than that she's got too much love
Not to share it around.

She'd be in the bottom class at school, not too bright
But right in the thick of the action
And enjoying every naughty minute of it!

She'd be your best mate who'd come and sit beside you
Just because she thought you looked sad
And could do with the company.

She'd turn up in fancy dress to every drinks party or hen night
Not always in the right place or at the right time,
But always the most enthusiastic.

She'd be the best babysitter and all the kids would love her
Because she'd sit quietly as they pulled her hair
And just look at you with big eyes as if to say, 'Bless them.'

She'd be one of those scruffy kids you hear mums shout at,
'Get your hair cut!'
And she'd give a warm, lopsided grin and say, 'Yeah, whatever!'

She'd always be first in line at the dinner queue,
Grab a huge bowl or two of whatever's on offer
And scoff it down in twenty seconds flat.

And she'd be the first person you invited to a sleepover,
All comfortable and cosy, loving and cuddly
Except for the snoring.

She's ten and acts like a five-year-old,
She's messy and noisy and always dirty,
She's Rosie and I love her.

Liz Nobbs

My Pet Dog

I love my little bulldog
And his silken, shiny cheeks,
I feed him on the choicest steaks
And expensive chocs for treats.
I take him to the local vet
And gladly pay the fees,
For the life of my pet doggie
Means the world and more to me!

Sometimes my maid is sulky
When I'm taking him for walks,
I can't help it if she's poor
And my pet dog eats choice pork
Because she doesn't matter
As much as darling pets to me,
And the life of little bulldogs
Should be as happy as can be.

She often gives me filthy looks
When for my dog she has to cook
A steak Diane or roasted quail
Haifa really is not worth her pay.
A refugee! An immigrant,
Is in no way equivalent
To friendly licks and scampering paws.

I wish that they would change the law
And send them back to where they're from
And import pekes and Dobermans
Who can speak in their sweetest talk
To rich pet owners, while they walk
And meet their friends, while all the wogs
Slave on their own in demeaning jobs.

Low pay, no rank, no hopes, no dreams
While me and doggie have a snoggie
By the Aga, sucking Imperial mint creams!

Angela Markos

Murphey

One day Murphey, a bearded collie cross whippet,
Was in need of a home, as his owners were returning to Spain.
He spent some time in quarantine before living here again
They felt after living in England, it would be too hot
So he needed a home and joined my lot.

Being born in Spain he has a short tail
A very happy dog tail wagging without fail
It starts wagging side to side
Then it goes round and round and back side to side.

The little dog known as a lurcher is happy all day long
And a joy to own that's for sure
Though he's not a pedigree, he is pure
Loving, affectionate, a comic to behold
Can't wait until the day his lead I will hold.

Then onto the parks for walks and fun
To the seaside for fun in the sun
Then tail wagging side to side and round and round
Happy days forever I'll be bound.

Joan Read

Purr-formance

I cannot speak your language,
but you say things loud and clear,
cosying around my legs
when dinner time is near.
Miaowing on the heart strings,
rattling at the door,
purr-ing to purr-fection
with eyes that ask for more.
Yours is the purr-fect language
to four paw through the day,
sleeping, eating, playing,
you go your purr-furred way!

Shirley Johnson

Creature Comforts

(In memory of my cat, Dandy)

I'm a fine-looking pussy who just needs his sleep,
So please don't disturb me when in slumber I'm deep.
I love the warm places where my people have been,
So their place on the bed is a choice spot to dream.

Insinuating myself in my mistress' place,
I miaow very loudly and pinch all her space.
My master warms up his own comfy chair,
Just the right temperature for me to sleep there.

I wait for my master to get out of my way,
Then jump up behind him, 'It's mine now,' I say!

I do love to sleep on a warm window sill,
The flowers are so pretty, so scented and still.
When the sun is too hot, my best comfort zone
Is under a bush to snooze all alone.

Whenever it's warm and soft to the touch,
You'll find me asleep, I love it so much.
The favourite place for my postprandial nap
Is cosily curled on my mistress' lap.

The cupboard for airing is the ultimate spot,
Please let me out now - I'm getting too hot!

Janet Lang

Just A Dog

There's a man with his dog across the street
Following closely near to his heels,
Doesn't have to look at the dog or speak
That dog knows just what his master feels.

The blind organist at our church has one too,
Throughout the service he lies still and quiet.
When the last hymn is announced, he knows,
Takes a walk round the church, he is so polite.

Oh what a wonderful animal is a dog,
Obedient, trustful and always alert.
Likes to lie across the hearthrug like a log,
Growls angrily when strangers are about.

A dog's an ideal pet for children at home,
He just loves to join in all their games.
Sometimes he will sit there like a garden gnome,
Enjoys running with them down country lanes.

A shepherd would be lost without such aid,
Just a whistle or two and it is understood.
It doesn't matter how the weather behaves,
His reward would be a good plate of food.

Albert E Bird

Smokey Jo

A kitten called Smokey Jo
Belly white, the rest dark grey.
Happy little soul to know
And enjoy seeing her play.

Mat-sliding on wooden floor,
Chasing golf balls down the stairs.
Stalking spiders near the door,
Jumping on and off chairs.

Bookcase climbing quite good fun,
Room behind books to hide in.
Chasing shadows in the sun,
Waving white paws at the bin.

Climbs up trees but can't get down,
Comes when shaking biscuit box.
A sweet little feline clown
Looks into shoes, dragging socks.

No more play, she needs a rest,
Circles round then finds the place.
Soft and warm, her little nest,
Often in a corner space.

Intelligent little pet,
A pleasure to watch her grow.
Her owner has no regret,
Only fun from Smokey Jo!

William Barnard

Cat-Apathy

Old Possum's Book of Cats, it is a book that I adore,
I read it hugging Tommy Tiddles lying on the floor.
It tells of Deuteronomy and Rum Tum Tugger too,
And the Grumbie Cat who, with some Beetles, made a fine tattoo.

It tells of Pekes and Pollicles and other feline gems,
It tells of rough Growltiger who's the Terror of the Thames,
Of Rumpelteazer, Skimbleshanks and one they call just Gus
And Jellicles when out at night, who kick up such a fuss.

Old Possum's Book of Cats is great, I hope you all agree
And I thought that Tommy Tiddles would feel the same as me,
But as I read he heaved a sigh and didn't move a paw
And when they found Macavity - he gave a little snore!

Peter Davies

My Three Moggies

Ollie's enormous and gives me a glare,
if his food's not on time, he thinks it's not fair.
He's as black as the night and never bothers to play,
in fact he lazes around, most of the day.

Little Tiger, he prances around on the sink
he knows it's an out-of-bounds place for a drink.
But if I scold him, he flies off and jumps on the chair
and sits and perceives me with a superior stare.

Gizmo, my third, hails from the back of beyond,
comes in and looks like he's swum in the pond.
He's a beautiful nature that much you can see
when I call him he leaps through the cat flap to me!

Jo Sparkes

Frankie Frog

On a rock beside the garden pond, sat Frankie Frog,
he was used to the clean luxury of life and couldn't stand anything which resembled a bog!
The pond had the cleanest water on which water lilies lie,
and Frankie didn't have to search far to catch the juiciest flies.
Frankie loved the early morning when the dew glistened on the grass
and around the pond, the birds sang out, such a sweet morning song . . .

Mary Plumb

He Found A Home

Thomas, the cat, hated the town
Often went away to hide,
His master said, 'We'll move away,
This place we cannot abide.'

Then came the day to move away
But Thomas could not be found,
Time did not wait, they had to go,
So Thomas was left around.

Now Thomas had no home at all,
And was all alone on his own,
But then a little girl came by
To take Thomas, the cat, home.

Now he lives in the countryside
With fields all around too,
He has found so many good friends
He can't believe it's so true.

So now he lives a happy life
And just lies about and sleeps,
So when the girl comes home from school
He comes out to have a peep.

Margaret Burtenshaw-Haines

Polar Bear

To be seen is quite rare
This large white polar bear
Global warming is the fear
As their feeding grounds disappear.

They need these to hunt and feed
To keep growing and breed
Melting snow and ice
Is their ultimate price.

The polar bear does not understand why
Humans only know why
Do we really care
As the polar bear becomes more rare?

Polar bears we must protect
They need our help and respect
To roam around the icebergs free
Or their likes we will never again see.

Garry Bedford

our cat, Rusty

Our lovely cat, Rusty
A loveable, large, long-haired Tom.
He's so friendly and trusty
A real family friend.
When in winter
It's cold, he'd always stayed in
Having a fuss made of him.
Sprawl out in front of the gas fire,
Sprawl there for hour, after hour,
Content warm and snug on his back,
Waiting for his belly to be rubbed
Like a sprawling warm ginger mat.

BG Clarke

Rescue Cat Awards

(Dedicated to Cats Protection and to my cat Tabby Tiger who was a runner-up in the first ever best friends category)

Suddenly, it's that time of year
When rescue cats bring good cheer
With tales of trouble, bravery and woe,
Those felines certainly put on a good show.

All their lives now saved and cherished,
By kind owners who would not let them perish.
The categories will break your heart,
Each story tho' provides a brand new start.

Last year Mitzi stole the prize,
Now it's the chance for one of you guys,
Survivor, traveller, character or friend,
Most amazing, even those on the mend.

I tried my paw out in the race,
Popular with the media for my cute face.
The mighty Tabby Tiger is my name,
Mum's now a poet, so we both found fame.

Best wishes to the Rescue Cat team,
I'm sure you all know who I mean.
I told my story and did my best,
Once again it's over to you to do the rest.

Good luck to one and all,
I know that in March you will have a ball,
Fat or thin, big or small,
Winners get ready to take your call!

Theresa M Carrier

Missing My Cat, Jenny

(Eleven days after being put to rest)

Alone I drink my coffee now,
No fur to feel, no soft miaow.
No touch for touch as we snuggle together,
No paw in hand as light as a feather.
Miss the purring high and low,
Miss the big green-eyed glow.
Miss you sitting on the stair,
Miss you curled under radiator there.
Miss giving you titbits, miss you so,
Miss you darting to and fro.
Miss you stretched in the midday sun,
Miss how the light made your colours run.
Miss you sharing dinner and tea,
Miss the marble eyes looking at me.
Miss you sharing my yoghurt too,
These miss you times are making me blue.
Miss patting you goodnight,
Miss seeing you at first light.
Missing you Jenny, my ginger tabby cat,
Miss those graces, that look of an aristocrat.

Vera Collins

Untitled

Big fat, hairy kitten
You lumpy ball of fur
You slice me with your gnoshers
And pin me to the chair.

There's mud and bits all over
And a whisker over there
You eat me out of house and home
And all you do is purr!

The problem with the cat flap
My nightly do or dare
Last night I was quite shocked to find
A mouse under the stair!

But life would be quite boring
If you were never there
I'm off to get more Iams
You big fat ball of hair.

Martin Colclough

Cry

I heard a cry, a chilling cry
A wolf nearby
An icy howl to freeze my blood;
Two red eyes and an icy grin
Piece this misty night,
Sending me all a-shiver,
Falling backwards into a river.

K M Clemo

Pooch

I wake in the morning to the scents on the breeze
For my kennel is open and does not need keys
My home's on a mountain surrounded by trees
I'm queen of my patch and all that I sees.

We've no near neighbours, my boss and I
Just acres of forest and hillside and sky,
I follow my nose and really do try
To find the places where the wildlife lie!

I have lived here for most of my life
Except for ten weeks with my father's wife.
Now I'm eight years old with little strife
My cares are few but the rain is rife.

Although I'm of Labrador and Spaniel mix
I'm not daft about rain - I'd rather do tricks,
The rain is OK but I'd rather chase sticks
When it's dry and dusty not pouring bricks.

I have a ball that's bouncy and red
I've chased it for miles as from the boss it's fled,
Cos he throws it for me so I earn my bread
And he doesn't have so far to tread.

So, above is my story - short as you see
But that's like my legs and they're part of me,
I'm happy and content just to roam free
With the boss, the hillside and occasional tree!

Alan R Coughlin

The Dog That Chewed Dad's Bowler Hat

The dog that chewed Dad's bowler hat
Really wasn't a dog, it was my cat
I found the brim, soggy, chewed and bent
And puss asleep in the crown, content.

When Dad came home that day from work
He blew his stack and he went berserk
His moustache quivered, his face went red
So next-door's dog got the blame, instead.

Dad raced next door in righteous huff
He dragged out the poor dog by his scruff
The dog reacted as well he might
With a scared yelp then a painful bite.

Things got wild, the dog chasing Dad
The neighbours arrived, boy were they mad
Sheer pandemonium, the noise, the din
Uproar so great the police were called in.

I'll never forget the look on Dad's face
When police caught the dog and ended the chase
When asked what had caused such a frightful scrap
Dad replied lamely, 'He's chewed up me hat!'

Dad limped back home, his dignity in shreds
Cops back to the station, neighbours to bed
That just left the dog and of course, the cat
Curled up together, asleep in the hat.

Andrew Renella

Bears

Shshshsh!
I am a polar bear who knows
That when I sleep - my nose gets froze!
But here's a funny thing
It gets thawed out in spring.

Shshshsh!
I am a koala bear who sleeps
In this eucalyptus tree I keeps!
Glad I'm here and not up there
Beside that frozen polar bear!

R Bissett

Sebastian - Number Nine

Sebastian is the end of the line,
I can hardly believe he's mine.
I thought the last was number eight,
But I really do believe in fate.

Superlatives defy description -
He is just absolute perfection,
A king of dogs with such a regal air
Sporting a figure with red golden hair.

It's such a joy to have him here,
He's happy, charming, such a dear.
I never thought I'd love again
With all the joy and maybe pain.

Ina Harrington

The Coalfinch

The coalfinch is a funny bird
Discovered the other day
It doesn't fly like other birds
It behaves in a peculiar way.
For whilst the gulls and robins
Go winging through the sky,
The coalfinch digs and burrows
Though there is a reason why.

For coalfinches are attracted
And beckoned by coal seams
They will not be distracted
Or put off by smokescreens.
And whilst the gulls and robins
Are dancing in the sun,
The coalfinch searches in darkness
For the prize that must be won.

So when next you burn a coal fire
Upon an English August day,
And you hear the sound of swallows
Chirping out most gay.
Think of the sturdy coalfinch
Missing the summer fun,
As it digs and burrows in darkness
For the prize that must be won.

Stuart Delvin

Samson

He is a Welsh Border Collie
Full of love and giving
He now is twelve years of age
But still is going on one
He loves his walks in the park
Chasing everything in sight
To come to heel is not too good
He has a mind of his own
Black and white with brown eyes
And a white tip at the tail
He bounds on his merry way
Making out that you're not there
A dog full of love and kindness
He nuzzles you when you're not well
And barks at some unlikely times
Until you say to him, 'Stop!'
He goes on his merry way
Leading his doggie dance.

Elaine Day

Cuckoo

In the fields in April
You would love to go,
For perchance you'll hear a bird
Singing sweetly just one word
Cuckoo! Cuckoo! Cuckoo!
Spring is here again,
Cuckoo! Cuckoo! Cuckoo!
Come and join the strain.

If you live in town
Or in city great,
Don't forget to listen
For the country treat.
Cuckoo! Cuckoo! Cuckoo!
You will hear her sing,
Cuckoo! Cuckoo! Cuckoo!
Don't you know it's spring?

So go into the country
Where the air is sweet,
Into peace and quietness
Away from bustling feet.
Cuckoo! Cuckoo! Cuckoo!
You will hear her voice,
Wouldn't you like to live there
If you had your choice?

Mabel Dickinson

Black Dog

Black dog running,
Scything through the grass;
Gloss-coat, sunshine-burnished.
Summers fade and pass.

Black dog streaking,
Arrow-straight in flight,
Through the tawny lanes of autumn,
The woodsmoke-scented nights.

Black dog leaping,
Drunk on spring and sun,
Racing, chasing, crazily
Dizzyingly young.

Black dog rolling,
Muzzled white with snow;
Wind-chill frosted whiskers.
Winters come and go.

Black dog passing,
A whisper on the breeze,
Stately, wise and solemn,
Into dreamful ease.

Black dog sleeping,
Untouched by rain or sun.
My heart is lying with you
Now your running days are done.

Aideen D'Arcy

Twin Kittens

Our daughter one day came home from work,
And said, 'A kitten I would like.'
We said, 'That's fine but only one.'
We knew what she was like!

The following day as home she came
A cardboard box she brought,
And there inside, guess what there was?
Two kittens, not one as we had thought.

'And why is this?' we deigned to ask,
'They would have been lonely if parted,' she said.
Her heart just melted where cats are concerned
And she placed them together in one little bed.

Our daughter has now grown up and moved on,
She now has a new little cat of her own.
Those twin kittens, they are now growing old
But she still likes to see them whenever she's home.

Iris Covell

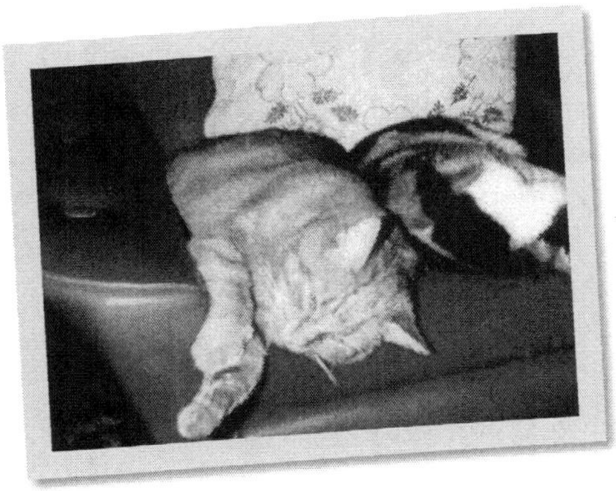

Monty

Monty the cat had a black eye
It was caused by a ginger tom
But he had pride and plenty of style
So he walked off with aplomb.
He had had many a fight
Usually over some female or another
Some of them liked to play the field
One even cheated on him with his brother.
Oh the tales that he could tell
And the battles he had won,
But he'd finally met his match
When in his street came the ginger tom.
Then one day when he was out
He came across a terrible sight,
Some toms were beating a lone cat
So he waded in with all his might.
He dispatched each one in turn
Then went to look at the injured cat,
But to his amazement he found
It was the ginger tom on the mat.
He helped him up and helped him home
But not a word was said,
He licked the wounds and cleaned the fur
And then put him to bed.
A week went by, then one day
The ginger tom paid him a call,
Thanked him for all he had done
And said they shouldn't fight at all.
Monty agreed and they shook paws
And Ginger told him his name,
Reaching this peace with ginger tom
Was to Monty his El Alamein.

Diana Daley

Ginger, The Library Cat

Ginger, the library cat, is always there,
So fat, heavily sprawled on a chair,
Always asleep, or seemingly so,
Except for the times you become aware
Of his enigmatic, green-eyed stare.

What a truly perfect life he leads
Never other than at his ease,
Rarely moving, except to amble
Leisurely around the adjoining garden.

Circling the plum tree, replacing the one
Under which, centuries ago a young, doomed poet,
Ravished by the song of a nightingale,
Memorably wrote a poem distilling its beauty
Of which, all of mankind is a beneficiary.

Does Ginger, the fat cat, know about that?
I doubt it and yet in the unfathomable
Depths of his emerald eyes there is something astir,
As if he too of such splendour may be aware.

Lynne Munn

Cherry Bough

Arise and court thou busy bee,
Buzz and buzz fantastically.
Beneath the sun, upon the breeze
Where creeping flowers catch the trees
And shires clip-clop their creaking wane,
Glorious in a blossomed lane.

Spin green as green a leafy tree,
As soft through branches heavenly
One pinking flower she yields thee now,
Here upon a cherry bough.

Oh I love thee, thou blushing maid
Beneath the cherry tree so laid,
And in her shade I ask of thee,
To disregard the sting in me...
And love me now as I love thee,
One pinking flower to yield me now
Here beneath the cherry bough.

Let pulchritude oust chastity,
And kiss me oh so verily,
For I, in very want of thee
Am now become a busy bee.

Roger Mosedale

My old cat

My cat she is old and tired
She is seventeen next birthday
She seems to be fine in her health although
She is a scruffy little shadow of her previous self
But her life is ebbing away
I shall miss her, what can I say?

She has been part of my life for seventeen years
Two children she has seen come into her life
They both love her and know of no other cat in their lives
Her eyes seem to be dim and she seems to be deaf
She still eats like a horse and drinks like a fish
She lies in the sunshine and enjoys her life.

When we moved house I feared the worst
A new place for her with her failing eyes
But she has coped extremely well.

She likes the garden, she didn't stray
She didn't try to run away
To go to the other place she knew
Where the furniture was what she was used to.

She was six weeks old and far too young
To be taken away from her mum
I shall miss her little paw
Resting on my shoulder at the top of the chair
'I love you Mum' it says to me
'Don't worry when I leave you
I will be ready'.

J Jannaway

My Budgie

Oh Monty, Monty, I taught you to talk
To mimic, wolf whistle and swear,
And now a day doesn't go by
That you don't pollute the air!

I can't invite posh relatives to stay,
You tell them in no uncertain terms,
You've had enough of their company
P*** off and never return.

You wolf whistle so loudly
That girls turn their heads in the street,
You sit on your perch so proudly
Why can't you be more discreet?

I never know when you will start
You swear at the most awkward times,
I'm always on edge, wondering what you will say
I wish you could forget the rude rhymes.

I started out thinking it so funny
But the joke has backfired on me,
If you were a child, I'd have no hesitation
Of putting you over my knee!

Susan Jenner

House Guests

Your balance is impeccable
Your head for heights supreme
Your breeding and your sense of taste
Are fine in the extreme

You drink the freshest water
And feast on best pâté
You walk with class and attitude
Such an elegant sashay

You only use the main entrance
Won't stoop to use the flap
You're partial to a broadsheet
If it's there on someone's lap

You drink full fat not semi-skimmed
Won't touch the coarsest meat
Though you like to try a little taste
Of everything we eat

You encourage us to do the chores
To work, to keep the house
You occasionally reward us
With a small but tasty mouse

You choose to live here just for now
We mustn't take as read
The honour that you grant us
When you let us share your bed

You're feisty and you're loveable
And you really like to chat
It's only really you that doesn't realise
You're a cat!

Nicola L Johnson

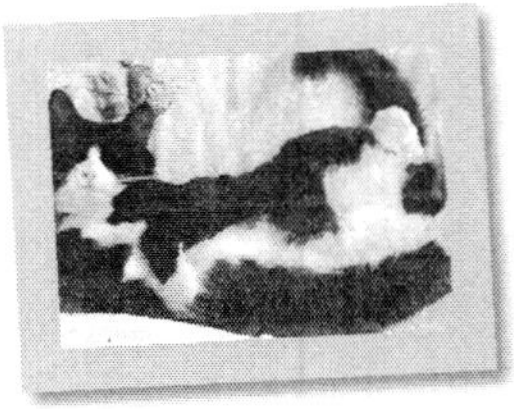

Cats

Cats cloud imagination
dropping in on little fog feet.
They flirt with wind,
ask questions of the snow
and worship sun
in supine arabesques.

Cats mate indecorously,
give birth immaculately,
discard on cue.

In caves, fire that lured cats
flickered on hunters drawn
as victors in the chase. Cats
learned of sympathetic magic.
They borrowed bones from birds,
tucked whispers into ears;
put pride in tails.

Was anything more honest than cats' eyes?
Did any animal so well pursue deception?

With wide receptive ears
cats listen hard
for anything to turn
to their advantage;
but veil the open archways of their minds
with long hairs curling in.

Eve said, 'It was a serpent
in the garden.' Certainly, it was smooth
and sinuous with wicked, wicked eyes
and sly, intrusive tongue
but I know (for Adam told me so)
it was the cat.

Jenny Argante

Make-Believe

I buy him new bones.
Ones of compressed hide -
flavoured in beef,
easy to hold, well contoured
and appropriately sized.

But he is not interested.
He carries it around
as cigar, dangling
between his teeth
or licks the ends
for a while, before making
half-hearted attempt
to rip off a chunk
bleeding gums.

Suddenly he gets up,
takes this perfect
artefact, buries it
in the garden,
amongst freshly laid lily bulbs,
so it won't be easy to find.

It would get all softened
and soiled.

He returns happy
as if he has won a game,
having failed many times
to catch a squirrel
or a bird alive.
Once he did catch a bird -
he was so startled,
he let go this life
to flutter away and fly.

Uma Asopa

My Dog

He would not go out if it rained,
We had to have him potty trained.
I don't know how this was achieved
Though from long walks I was relieved.
For lesson two he had to train
And get the knack to pull the chain
A difficulty in this issue
Involved the use of toilet tissue
This plan would be complete of course
When he had learned to wash his paws.
Stretching things beyond belief
Is expecting him to brush his teeth.
Then as he grew he soon was able
To join us at the breakfast table.
I wish our Fido then could talk
Of how he used a knife and fork.
Many owners must have yearned
For their doggie to have learned
Then they could do the same as me
Loll about and watch TV.
Now on TV I watch old talkies
There is no need to go out walkies.

Bill Austin

Cats

Who'd have cats? They drive you spare
their grubby paws get everywhere,
they claw the couch and have to be
the only cat sat on your knee.

They haul their trophies through the door
then wonder what you're shouting for,
they'll proudly offer half a mouse
or drag dead sparrows round the house.

They eat and sleep and chase and fight
and caterwaul all through the night,
they howl for milk and only eat
their most expensive cuts of meat.

They cough up hairballs then they chew
a rare exotic plant or two
and scale tall heights in search of bees
but end up getting stuck in trees.

Treat next-door's garden as a loo
and yet, despite the things they do
how different my world would be
without a cat or two or three!

Their antics brighten up my day
and soothe my worries far away,
with each contented purr and miaow
I couldn't part with mine, could you?

Kathryn Atkin

Our Dog, Shandy

It was his eyes -
they spoke,
laughed, wondered, worried
they showed love.

House dog.
Men quailed at the sight
of teeth bared and white -
waiting, warning
but a gentle word
calmed him and thanked him
for his care.

Yes, it was his eyes
deep brown pools of love,
they were the last to go.
His body succumbed to age
but in the end
despite their trust
they had to close.

Remember the love in those eyes,
he asked for nothing but love.
Remember that,
and the gift of his love
will sustain us in his loss.

P Allen

Crommy, My Felis Silvestris

Colourful butterflies were fluttering
In middle of them, in long grass hiding
My little Crommy was happily playing
The next sight of him was his long tail
In purple jacaranda trees standing
Marvellous birds in myriad of shade
Birds of paradise, canaries, he was chasing
Strangely, he loves the scent of the flowers
And sometimes, in fragrant jasmines hedge
A nice little nap he was having
With his cheetah-like stride, he is a graceful mover
And his appearance is just striking
He has a pretty face with the M on the forehead
With a delightful personality, he is fascinating
He is fiercely loyal and has a great devotion for me
His amber-gooseberry eyes are piercing
He is a feline of tremendous strength
But he communicates in soft melodious voice by chortling
He is kind, shy, clever and very proud
But he loves to come near me purring
He adores the heat of the sun
But doesn't like too much when it's raining
My adorable, handsome, athletic mini-tiger
Now, in luxury of our home where you are living
Little Felis Silvestris, you deserve all our loving.

John Stubbs

Ill-Met By Moonlight

The evening smoulders, hums with heat,
And the cat sneaks into the bedroom at my feet
Like a tacked-on shadow. He loves the magic of cold air
Running through his coat,(it's a mystery) after a long day
Spent panting, flung on tiles like a skinned rabbit,
And lies wedged between my ankles, paw over eyes;
We both know this entente will not last. I will be
Sunk dead, eyeballs flickering behind closed lids
And my weightless mermaid self flowing with a luminous tide,
Just as he wakes flustered from his first dream, encountering
His feral self in a moonlit labyrinth. The wild red night cat
Bares teeth, scolds him, hissing, for selling out, for getting soft,
Sleeping on soft sheets while his wild family is out hunting,
Lured on through tawny grass by twitterings and hunger.
It's then the night goes awry: he drops softly to the floor
Driven by insatiable bloodlust and clawstrophobia,
Half-sheathed claws click as he corners at speed,
Bone knocks on wood like cricket ball on suicide fielder,
Vase rocks, echoing, on table, rugs get folded like pastry,
And I wake groaning, stagger to the door and he's gone.

Liz Davies

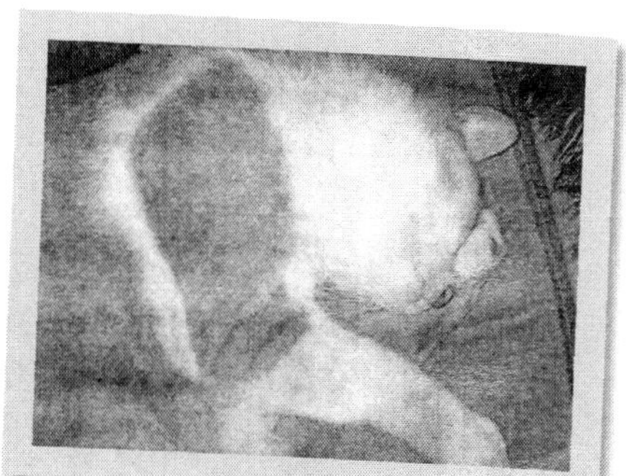

Zebra Finch

Phweep! Jump left, jump right,
Small black eyes, blinking rapidly,
Orange beaks this way and that way,
Hop up, hop down. *Phweep!*

An egg cracks and shows a tiny lump of grey flesh
Phweep! Little tufts sprout from head and breast,
Eyes just swollen blobs above
A miniature beak, forever open. *Phweep!*

Back and forth from perch to perch
White feathers, grey feathers, make this nest the best
Phweep!
A chick so small, though warm and fed
Its tiny heart no longer beats.

Phweep! Parents hysterical. *Phweep!*
Not understanding where they went wrong
Back and forth, up and down
Left and right. *Phweep! Phweep!*
Knowing it's too late and nothing can be done.

A large hand thrusts into the cage and removes the tiny form.
Phweep! Phweep! Where has our child gone?
A human tear drops in the nest as the chick is gently taken
And carefully buried with others and quietly named and laid to rest.

Phweep! Phweep! Back and forth and left and right
Up and down, another twig, more straw and hay,
White and brown feathers. Make this nest the best!
Another egg laid. *Phweep!*
Keep it warm, keep it covered
And hope again once more.

Julie Phelan

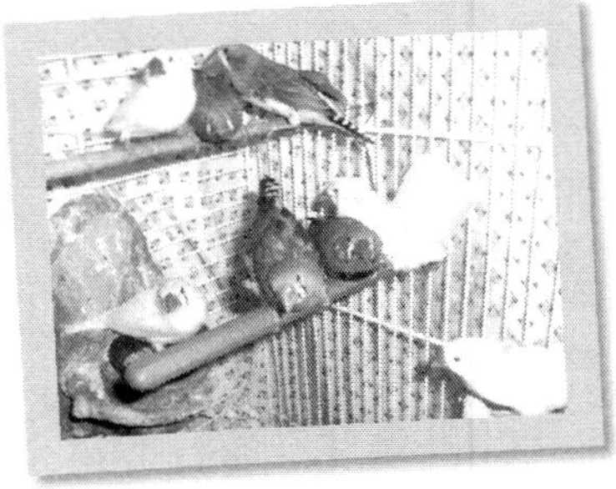

Tiger, Tiger

Tiger, tiger, walks along the stream,
Flashing your eyes in the moonbeam.
Brushing your stripes along the tree bark
Hearing the sweet song of the lark.
Tiger, tiger, swimming in the lush lagoon
To hunt his supper he will go soon.
Out of the lagoon he prowls
To stun his prey he makes a low growl.
Tiger, tiger, leap out on a deer which is your prey
But landing in a heap of hay
Though holding the neck of his prey which makes his day
He's very cunning as others say.
Into his dreaded lair
He is deadly but he looks fair
His lair isn't too far
Eats his dinner then sleeps under the North Star.
But numbered his days are
We humans have gone too far,
If people do not stop this
The tiger is a creature we will miss!

Karishma Porwal

Love Hurts

At last I know she loves me
Though it's taken fifteen years.
And throughout that time together -
We've shared joy and fun and tears.

I chose her in adoption
And held her to my heart,
Knowing she was the one for me,
From the very start.

Yet sometimes, I did feel a doubt
If she loved me true;
For when another came along -
I felt she loved her too.

But now I know it's proven,
Although I spat and hissed,
As she injected me it hurt -
Then gave a tender kiss.

The tears were flowing from her heart,
Her nerves in tattered shreds,
Lying awake for long, long hours
As life hung by a thread.

That was the first of many -
When she plunged into my skin,
A needle with the sharpest point,
To deliver insulin.

Now I know she saves my life
Each morning when we rise;
So I give her many extra purrs -
A mature cat is very wise.

Anita Richards

Untitled

Through good and through bad times,
Through rain and through shine,
Through love and through heartbreak
You've always been mine.

Through sun and through winter,
Through summer and fall,
Through laughter and sad times
You've been there through all.

I come home on cold nights,
You're sat at my door,
I come home on hot days,
You're there, who could want more.

We have such a short time
On Earth, you and I,
But I'll love your for all time,
Until the day that I die.

Cassandra Lennon

A Day of My Cat Angel

As we awake a life downstairs is purring up our chairs
As her big green eyes glitter in the darkness like diamonds
The attention-seeking cat lies down comfy on her mat.
As we get ready she's still like a teddy
Suddenly a slam, she's alone once again.
The cold air blows as she sees the window wide open
A jump, in a flash she is on the other side of the wall.
As she squeezes her tiny head through the garden gate
Where her brother Sam awaits
They run and have fun chasing the flies.
Suddenly a car, she knows her family's back
She runs like the wind aside the car
Then follows us up to the door.
Inside, a saucer of Whiskers, fine food awaits her needs
She gobbles and gulps it down fast
And jumps onto the owner's lap watching the fire burn.
One eye closes slowly until she is once again reunited with her soft pillow.

Abigail Webb

One Airedale For Sale

Named Millie, or Millie Mollie Mandy as she is sometimes referred to.
Minus two claws
Half house-trained
I'm guessing you know which end to keep outside
A bit fussy
Gets PMT often, not joking!
Hates being clipped
She is the boss.

Any offers?

Gemma-Jaine Field

Haven's Peace

God bless the animal shelters
And the people that are kind
For without their help and devotion
God knows what you would find.
Praises for the vets that used their healing hands,
Helpful, useful nurses, poorly pets to understand
Neglected pets aren't funny
So sad these dilemmas exist
A pet must get attention
With love and food not missed.

Angela Allen

Tzara

My Russian royalty.
The Tzar of Russia had a gruesome death,
my Tzarina lives on in bushy fur
ruling with a timid grace.
Miaow, she protests,
it's not a suggestion.
Mottled white, ginger, black,
four white gloves ready for inspection
because the food is too dry,
she prefers peppermint tea,
the scent of +a swimmer's hair,
or a manufactured bag to tear apart.
And after that she will proceed to make her mark
with furballs and claws on the sofa;
a cat's Hollywood walk
each mark a star of her monarchy.
And though she'd never brag
her tail makes the perfect regal flag.

Emma Parfitt

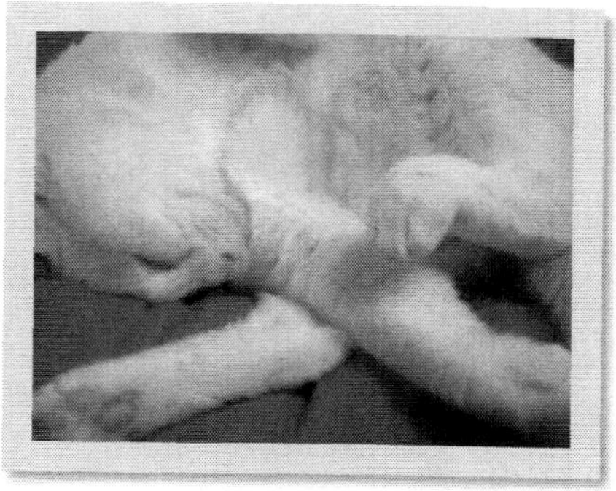

Without You

What am I going to do with all this time without you?
You were an old dog, nearly blind and deaf
But you gave me through your life
So much love, so much loyalty
Anything I did, your adoring eyes
Were following me everywhere
When you were able, we walked every day
You loved so much your nice walks
In sunshine, in rain, even in snow
With your little red coat protecting you
In the house, you were following me everywhere
I nearly fell on you so many times in my kitchen
You slept in my bedroom in your cosy bed
When you were unable to walk, I carried you
For everybody you were an old soft dog
But for me, you were my mate, my real friend
At the end you were suffering too much
We had to let you go for your best
Losing you is so much to bear, it really hurts
We love you little Louis and miss you so much
I heard to a place named Rainbow Bridge
Where you are waiting for us
When it will be my turn, we will cross this bridge
I will follow you in this dog paradise
Looking in your trusting eyes
Never to be parted again in this wonderful place
Where cocker spaniel goes to Heaven.

Victorine Lejeune Stubbs

Socks

His gentle paws paved the way
Yes, he's come once more
From early morn to late at night
He crouches by that door

He is not ours, he just appeared
Just a little kitten
We watched him grow, he was so sweet
By him we all were smitten

He's black and white with four white paws
That's how the name was born
His real name is Basil
Which left us all forlorn

I remember when he climbed that tree
In the garden shade
Once when he got up so high
Coming down he was afraid

His antics keep us laughing
He follows us around
That little cat when he appears
Spreads happiness around.

Andrea Lynne Taylor

Trix, Then And Now

I never knew when I first saw you
A tiny baby in a heap,
That you and me would have a future.

I took your brother, frail and small,
From your pile of sibling love,
But the father took him from me.

When I returned, you had grown,
And I removed you from your huddle,
But your brother still stayed with me.

You took his name but you were strong,
Stronger than he was
And you were my companion.

When I stop and look back now
I see you in your glory,
Back when you were a vibrant life.

Now those glinting, ruby eyes
That once held life and vigour
Are dulled with years of age.

And your soft white coat
Is dusted with marks
And grows in wiry tufts.

A form that was once strong and lithe
Lies curled and trembling
In almost permanent sleep.

And limbs that held your little form
So steady in their day,
Drag behind you like dead weights.

I remember and love you in your forgotten youth
And though your body lies decrepit
I dread the day you leave me, my little Trix.

Charlotte Singleton

Fred, The Fish

I was feeling very sad, you see, I'd lost a chum
His name was Fred, he was multicoloured
I was like his mum

Freddie was no ordinary fish, he was such a clever chap
I used to teach him cunning tricks
To jump into my lap

Then Fred and I, we had a tiff, he said that he would leave
I thought he'd just gone to sulk
Why was I so naïve?

I went to all the fishy hangouts that Freddie used to like
I even scoured the banks of rivers
But all I saw were pike

Then one day my friend, Mike, came round for a cuppa
He thought that (to cheer me up)
He'd take me out to supper

We went to the local chippy, I ordered 'Fish of the Week'
The food came, and through the breadcrumbs
I managed to take a peek...

And then I saw the fish-skin colour my stomach turned to lead
The fish that I was about to chomp
Was none other than my Fred!

I shouted at the waiter and screamed, 'I refuse to pay!'
The waiter said, 'Please madam calm down
Or they'll all want one, won't they?'

Louise Hawker

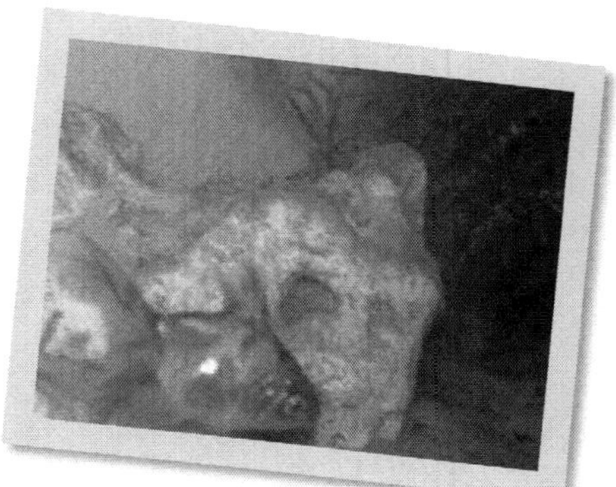

The Great Puppy-Feet Escape

Bert's his name, and sniffing his game,
All other names forsaking;
And when the back door opens up
He sets about escaping.
At first he sits there quietly looking
Timid, docile and shy,
And all the while he's staring at you
With his beady eye.
As soon as you have gone from sight
The boundaries he will scan,
Testing with his keen wet nose
And working out his plan.
He ran away three times before
But then we rescued him
The last time, caught him round some flats
With another dog called Tim.
But here he lives, and here he stays
Still looking for a way
To trot off on his puppy feet
And do the town for a day.
I'm sure that one day he might make it
Sneaking through the gate,
And probably scamper down to the flats
And look for Tim, his mate.

Stephen Chering

Jimmy Direct

(A narrative poem)

He stood tall
All sixteen hands of horse-power
A rangy brown colt
Black mane and tail
Long pointed ears
Huge dark eyes
Looking out warily
On an uncertain world.

Reared by some gipsies
His home the grass verge
By the roadside
His sire a trotter
Dam unknown
Sold for ten pounds
To a pony-trekking centre
Racing in his nature
Bred to win
Always in the lead was Jimmy Direct

Wintered out to a family
A treat for the children
'Don't work him too hard,' they said
'Needs a bit of feeding up,' they said
So Jimmy came to us.

Broken-in too early
As yet to grow into his gangling legs
'Keeps his distance,' they said
'Needs a bit of petting,' they said.

Jimmy lying down
In the sweet grass of the orchard
Nibbling the windfalls
That came his way.
Eager for the titbits
He gradually learned to take
From our outstretched hands
Stroking the velvet-softness of his nose

Leaning against him
Our arms round his neck.

Jimmy trotting
Faster than the wind
Black mane and tail
Streaming out behind
We learned him to canter
Through the seat of our pants
A clumsy, rollicking gait
'That an Injun pony you got there?'
The local lads shouted after us.

When the time came
To fetch him home
He wouldn't go in the horsebox
Without a slap and a threat
And a jerk on the reins
'You've spoiled him,' they said
Jimmy would never be the same again.

They sold him to a riding school
For two hundred and fifty pounds
He'd be all right there
With the children all around
And he'd always be out in the front
Would Jimmy Direct
I'll never forget you
Jimmy Direct.

Beryl Johnson

Jackson, The Jack Russell

Before Jackson came into our lives we liked everything just so,
Choosing designer cushions in pastel shades coordinating with silk throws.
Now we search for things that don't show the hairs and fabrics that won't stain,
Going on early morning *walkies*, have we gone a little insane?
I'm gazing at the object of our devotion, who gazes equally devoted in return,
So when I think of our lives pre-Jackson, it seems we had much to learn.
'Okay, we'll have some ground rules, not on the furniture or on the bed.'
Now as I notice him snuggled in the cushion pile, was that really what I said?
And that statement, 'For holidays he won't tie us down, into kennels he must go.'
But could we leave him there with strangers? I think the answer is no!
As I'm writing this I'm smiling, pondering on how our lives he has changed about
However, don't hold me in derision, get a dog, you'll soon find out!

Eileen Wilby

My New Pup

My lovely dog, she suddenly died
My heart was broken, I cried and cried.
The phone it then went, a voice on the line
Said, 'Please can you help
I haven't much time?
I have a young pup in need of a home
Her owners were cruel and she's nowhere to go.'
So I agreed again to start
To help this pup and mend my heart.
I put out my arms, I welcomed you here
I built up your trust, I helped chase the fear.
You soon came around and started to be
A happy young pup, safe and carefree.
You chewed my shoes, pulled sheets off the line,
Sneaked into my room, made it yours and mine.
You barked at the postman, you chased the cat,
You lay on the sofa, you ate the mat.
But the love you gave for all your mishaps
More than made up as you sat on my lap.
And I am so glad, I answered the phone
And agreed to let you come live in my home.

Monica McNamee

Simbo

Simbo is a budgie
A clever little chap
He trots right through his ladder
And the wire his beak will tap.

He loves to chatter quickly
And flies about his cage
He wags his chin and nods his head
As if he's in a rage.

Simbo is a show off
He can turn head over heels
He ties himself into a knot
And then he eats his meals.

He sits and watches all we do
And signs his songs with glee
He gives us hours and hours of joy
So full of life is he.

When the day is finished
He climbs onto his swing,
He rocks until his eyes are closed
And we know Simbo's sleeping.

E Blackburn

Tusk

Looks like they're on a trip, safari, vacation,
looks like they're on a hunt.

We see them every year,
bushmen and their pale companions,
expedition bloodthirsty.

They murdered our ancestors,
woolly mammoth
and now they want to take us too.

Black market tusks for sale
and everyone just watches us die.

J A Carter

Teddy

He travelled well
caged like an extravagant notion
burning inside an introvert.
His feathers seldom ruffled
always preening and nipping the white edge
of cuttlefish bone fitted into its cage.
I grew up with him like a favourite book at bedtime
or kind-hearted uncle playing and watching him fly a-
round the living room strafing the coastline of my head
and lifting skyward up into the floral backcloth,
always interesting although as delicate as a sheet of ricepaper to touch.

Laurence De Calvert

A Pony's Tale

Hi folks, my name is Truffles,
I'm a dark brown Shetland pony you see.
Dad bought me for when the grandchildren came
Took me home to the Willows on Lordship Lane.

I had my own little paddock and shed
On water and hay and carrots I fed
And of course I grazed on the sweet green grass.

I was happy at Wistow and spoiled, oh my
The people came out when I was walked by
Gave me fruit and biscuits and stroked my head,
Let me graze on their lawns, oh I was well fed.

Children came to see me when I was at home
Dad and David cared for me, I was never alone.
I loved to give the grandchildren rides
Little Reece, Tom and Kelly with David as guide.

Dad kept chopped up carrots in his pocket for me
Sometimes he took some for Mum to give me
She was indoors, she's disabled you see.

David looked after me when poor Dad passed on
Had me fitted with shoes, brushed my coat till it shone.
He trained me to a little cart, though I say it myself, I did look smart.

He took me round the countryside, Tom and Kelly loved to have a ride.
All went well until my plight, I was out in my paddock late one night
When bangs and flashes way up high and bits that fell down from the sky.

I broke down my fence, I was so afraid
To escape from that horrible firework raid
I galloped and galloped into the night, till I was lost and shaking with fright.
I collapsed in a field, oh miles from home where I lay soaking and gasping for breath
Till daylight when a man came by walking his pets.

He hurried to tell some folks at a farm who came with a trailer and took me to their home.
They put me in a stable and tried to make me warm
I was covered with a blanket and hugged by a kind lady's arm.
David was out on his bicycle as soon as he knew I was gone,
My friends from the village were out searching too to bring me back where I belong.
Some men from the farm found David told him to come quickly to me,

As quick as he could, to my side he came
But I could never go back to Lordship Lane
I know I've been loved and always will be
When a big lad like David was crying for me.

Joan Lawson

A Letter To God

Dear God, Lord of all Heaven above,

I am writing to You amongst the uncontrollable burning tears that only accompany a broken heart, to humbly ask for Your love to watch over my beloved dog. You see, yesterday, against her will and mine, my dog was forced to go and live with You and Your kind.

I know full well she'll just sit by Your gates, watching the horizon, just knowing she's to wait, and not bearing me a grudge for being so late, but rejoicing the day she can run to my side, again wash my face and look deep in my eyes.

I too will be waiting, waiting for the day I can embrace her tightly, burying my face into her soft shiny coat, breathing in deeply her wonderful warm aroma, as overwhelming tears of joy roll down
my cheeks.

My dog and I will be whole again, not half. To wander as one, wherever our hearts desire. Through shady woods leading to sweet-scented meadows, where birds sing all around us. Once again, we can laugh and play in the streams like two children without a care, and lie down to rest in the cool shade of a tree. Lost in thought, watching the clouds drift slowly by, with my hand resting gently on her side. Both of us knowing nothing ever again can part us... together forever.

But until then Lord, if she's looking unhappy, or feeling low, please reassure her and let her know, one day I shall run to her, from over the horizon and relieve You of Your temporary job, of hugging and loving and watching over my most wonderful dog.

Thank You my Lord
A grieving dog owner
Earth.

Amanda Hawes

Bath Time

Shampoo and towels, I know what that means
I like to smell but they want me clean.
Buckets of water are put in a tub
I'm put in next and given a scrub.
After I'm rinsed I give a good shake
What a fuss my owners make.
Then I'm wrapped in a towel to dry
For the life of me, I don't know why!
Tomorrow they'll take me back down the lane
And I'll jump in the ditch and get smelly again.
Now I'm so tired I shut my eyes
They give me a hug with knowing sighs.

R Manning

Barney

I have a dog who's black and white, Barney is his name,
He's sometimes very naughty but I love him just the same.
He loves to play and dash about, acting like a fool,
And sometimes Mummy brings him to meet me out of school.
We take him for some lovely walks, where other dogs he meets
He's on his best behaviour too; he knows he'll get a treat.
And when he gets his little treat, he offers up a paw
Then he sits there, just waiting, hoping he'll get more.
He likes a little cuddle and sometimes he will lick us,
Then off he'll go into his bed, showing off his knickers.

Phyllis Sandiford

Cuthbert or Cuffy?

Cuffy has had to be put to sleep
he was a very old pussycat.
Over four years he's been with us
and went from very thin to very fat!
He was a down-and-out dustbin waller and lousy into the bargain!
His fur was dirty, people had thrown him out, what a sin.
We called him Scruffy at first but with careful attention and food
we changed it to Cuthbert, then Cuffy.
Scruffy was far too rude.
We brushed his coat until it shone and powdered him profusely.
He ate funny things, macaroons, cheese and would you believe muesli?
He liked being clean and kept himself washed and told us his desire.
He liked certain biscuits, certain food and a special place by the fire.
My job was so easy, after that, he took only minutes to groom.
Every day I miss him terribly, there's an emptiness in every room.

Ann May Wallace

Scooby Too

A Bernweiler lodger have we,
we thought he'd dropped in just for tea.
He's so gentle and kind,
yet his size blows your mind,
but we love him regardless you see.

He's so handsome and called Scooby Too,
a cross between Snowdog and Pooh.
An over-grown pup,
we just can't give him up,
so what do we do? What to do?

He says he'll be quiet as a mouse,
can he only remain in our house.
We really are all badly smitten,
with this giant who behaves like a kitten,
who's clever and uses his nous.

A big bed's appeared in the lobby,
it seems that we have a new hobby.
So the die has been cast,
Scooby's settled at last,
quietly snoring and crooning like Robbie.

Pat Williams

My Dog

Why do we find that our dogs are such good company?
I look around this local park and everywhere I see
Fellow pet lovers seemingly at peace with the world
With all their dogs alongside them as mine now is to me.

The ball is thrown and with joyous bark
Pets are off in pursuit, bounding along in great glee.
Then scampering back for it once more to be thrown
So pleased to please them, as mine is pleased to please me.

At home by the fireside he will sit at my feet
I'm sure he understands every word that I say
Oh not the language that's true, but the tone and timbre
He will sense my mood, be it filled with joy or dismay.

In my times of great sadness he's always been there
His head on my lap and brown eyes seeming to say
You and I will get through this, come on, give me a stroke
Let my presence here take your burdens away.

A dog is forever if you just treat him kind
That's all he asks for the love he will return
Your life will be enriched by the trust he has in you
And you'll find the contentment for which you so yearn.

Don Woods

Hope

I'm just an ordinary doggy
with lots of love to share,
all I want is a family
to give me love and care.
A nice little bed
and somewhere I can play,
some food, water
and love every day.
For in return, I will give to you,
a friendship to last forever,
a friendship that is true.
I will never leave you,
I'll stay by your side,
I'll look upon you as my master,
you'll see it in my eyes.

L Wilson

The Gypsy Pup

He came to me, the gypsy pup,
So frightened and forlorn.
I wondered at the 'sense of man'
Who let this pup be born.

I loved him from than moment
And as the weeks went by
My little pup just grew and grew
To over two feet high!

He'd turned into a lurcher
So full of life and zest,
Who sleeps with my Jack Russells
Like a cuckoo in the nest!

Elaine Francis

Dog Delight

I sauntered, lonely, feeling sad,
for things had not been going well,
with future prospects looking bad,
I felt depressed as one could tell.

Jus then, a little dog ran up
with wagging tail and eager eye.
He wasn't much more than just a pup.
To lick my face he had a try.

He must have sensed I was a friend,
for jumping, wriggling in delight,
he knew on me he could depend,
and wagged his tail with all his might.

Such joy and love bestowed for free,
I was a pal, that's all he cared,
I didn't deserve, goodness me,
but loving friendship was declared.

He sent my spirits rising high
and also made me give some thought
to those I'd helped in days gone by
who, my existence, quite forgot.

This little dog's love, freely given,
in gratitude, for just a pat -
compare with those for whom I'd striven
and never had a thanks at that!

Alan Wilson

Dodger

Dear Dodger you were saved from death
Thanks to that wonderful Forward Press
They gave you back your life to enjoy
You are such a brave little boy.
You look so happy now on your photos
What you have gone through no one knows
And you have such a sweet little face
We think that you are ace.
You will make someone happy
No doubt about that,
To someone who will love you
And you will love them.
A happy and contented life
I wish for you
And all that you dream about
Will always come true.

May Ward

Man's Best Friend

She never asks for anything and yet she's always there
Listens to my troubles, always seems to care,
If I'm happy, full of fun or maybe feeling blue,
She'll sit right down beside me; she knows just what to do.

To bring a smile upon my face, her face so full of care,
No need to thank her for her help, it's natural to her,
She's always there when needed, excepts nothing in return,
All help is given freely, nothing for me to earn.

Fifteen years of caring, loving me and still,
The best friend I have ever known, the only one I will,
She wanted nothing but my love, a love I gave so true
I miss my little waggy tail and I always will love you.

Kathleen Townsley

Life Loves

When I wake up in the morning
You are lying there,
You come and cuddle up to me
And sniff my ruffled hair.

Then it's down for breakfast
You go out to the loo,
While I am having tea and toast
You have your doggy goo.

It's time now for your walkies
You're gazing up at me,
We'll stop at every lamp post
So you can sniff and wee.

What would I do without you?
You're always there for me,
I cannot imagine how my life would be
Without my best friends.

AG Trick

George

I had a cockerel, his name was George
He was white and his comb so red.
His eyes bright brown and he'd strut around so grand.
Yet never ever once did he peck me,
I'd hold him in my arms and people would be shocked!
Each night he came to meet me just so I could put him in his safe wooden house.
He always waited at the gate, should I be late!
The other birds would safely go in, yet he waited in the cold and dark.
A happy cluck and into my arms he'd jump
'You're getting heavier George,' I said.
So that last night I put him to bed, his bright eyes looked up at me.
In the morning I went to open the birds up but he never came to me
And the other birds were looking down from their perches
At their old friend who lay so still by his perch.
For in the night George had died.
Don't know why? His heart maybe.
He was at his best, feathers so grand and comb so red, strong yellow legs to strut around.
How I shall miss the white cockerel waiting at the garden gate to say goodnight.

Jennifer Trodd

Deepest Disgrace

I'm bored and lonely and sad
I can't go home now, I've been really bad.
So I've scared all the bees off the flowers
And I've been watching this insects for hours
There's not much left for a poor cat to do
Except jump down and chase the odd shrew.
Now, I'm hungry as a hunter can get
But today, I'll never get fed you can bet.
I'm in the deepest disgrace
No way can I dare show my face.
I've got to sit here as long as it takes
'Til they forget that I've eaten the cream off the cakes!

Carol Spencer

Devoted Dog

If there's a dog within your home
You'll never ever dine alone
There's one thing you can guarantee
He'll come and keep you company
He doesn't drink so he'll decline
Your offer of a glass of wine
But just because he's your best mate
Takes anything from off your plate
He looks at you imploringly
He's had nothing all day you see
Like a Wimbledon spectator
Follows each fork of meat or tater
Whilst you dine in total thrall
Ignoring postmen should they call
For each morsel he'd sell his soul
Abandon jazz for rock 'n' roll
As you make your final swallow
Makes a date same time tomorrow.

John Smurthwaite

Miss Simpson

There's my small friend, stretched out in the sunlight.
But with one eye open a slit to watch the world.
Alert to any chance of attention, she shows her delight
And pleasure with a contented purr.
All our loving, brushing and talking,
Is returned to us a thousand fold.

As she joins us in a survey of her garden,
I wonder, how did she suddenly get so old?
Fifteen long years, her lifetime, she stayed
A comfort through my loss and pain.
I brought her home and gently laid
Her, stretched out in the sunlight, she loved, again.

E Davies

Pet Celebs And Dodger

There are famous dogs like Lassie,
K-9 and Rin Tin Tin
TS Elliot's cats and Felix
The Cheshire cat with a grin.

Celebrity pets of all kinds
Yet it is plain to see
That people also like to have
A nice bit of rough like me.

I'm rather photogenic
But modest with it too,
Not too large for the small car
A people's pet all through.

Kathleen M Scatchard

Axolotl

A presence in the room
The monster of the deep
The creature of dark waters
Sits in the tank
Regarding the ceiling
As he sits still
In quiet contemplation
Expressionless face
Inscrutable stare
Speaking volumes
As small eyes
See in front
In the wait for prey
And the mouth is fast
When prey appears
And yet another worm
Will disappear inside
Its cavernous body
While below
Or the insect in unwary pose
That falls upon the surface to struggle
The monster will get it from below
Jaws at the ready to engulf
From the deep
And what drives this creature
Member of an ancient race
Standing and watching the world.

Alasdair Sclater

Gifts

Thank you for your presents,
    you are a clever boy!
They're gifts to show you love me
    and I should be full of joy

But worms upon the carpet
    and dead spiders on the bed,
and growling from the hallway
    as you munch that beetle's head

Are not the kind of offerings
    designed to fill my heart,
with warmth and admiration
    for my young feline sweetheart

And can anything prepare me
    for the terror you'll arouse,
when proudly you trot up to me
    and give me your first mouse?

Tony Gardner

Feline Friends

In our house every day
Lots of cats come to play,
Through the cat flap, in the door
Enter lots of fur and claws.

Smokey's ours, a short-haired male,
Dark smoke grey from head to tail
With a rich deep bushy fur
And a lovely squeaky purr.

Then came trouble aplenty -
When Squeak from number twenty
Came to us to hide away
So the puppies there could play.

She's big for a female cat
And I think on top of that
She was always planning
To keep warm on the landing.

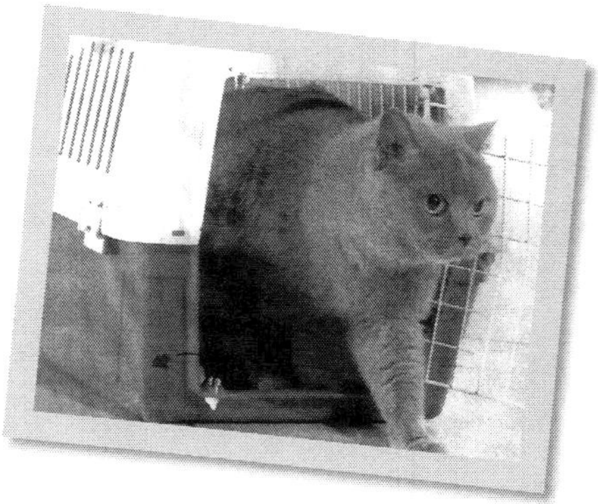

Smokey and Squeak made amends
And became the best of friends,
So much so Rachel thought that
We had got ourselves *two* cats!

Rob and Rachel moved next door
And Chan came to show a paw,
Short for Chandon, we did find
Part of France for making wine.

From her kitchen window seat
Chan would tend to do a leap,
Dainty darting to and fro
Is the way that she would go.

She would often spend her time
With me hanging on the line
All the washing to go out
Till Squeak made her want to shout.

Alas, time's passed and no more
Cats come squeezing through the door,
Sparky's still at twenty-six

Squeak seems to have lost her tricks.
It's no more a pussy Heaven
Two cats instead of seven,
Lots have passed on to sleep
Memories of them we keep.

Anne Lever

Jenkins

Sleeps on a cushion, contented and fat
This is Jenkins, our marmalade cat.
Can't out-run a rabbit, and won't catch a mouse
Blinks at the sunshine and won't leave the house.

He snoozes and twitches and dreams moggy dreams
Of soft beds and warm fires, cat food and cream.
In his dream heaven of all cats he's king,
With all of the luxuries kingship can bring.

When he's awake, though, his life's just the same
Pampered and spoiled since the day that he came
To live in our household, contented and fat,
This is Jenkins, our marmalade cat.

Merilyn Hill

Bad Luck

We thought we would walk dog along the beach
Area where not many tourists reach,
It was dusk and on the water lights shone
With a big splash, the dog had run, was gone!

Quickly she straight away turned and raced back
Escorted by sound of approaching quack,
Oh no! she'd disturbed family of ducks,
Poor old thing! We laughed, what dreadful back luck!

Now to seaside, dog's reluctant to go,
No matter what weather, sun, rain or snow.
Mention ducks, hides her head under her paws
Barking, *they're about, I'm staying indoors.*

S Mullinger

I Know Why The Caged Cat Sings (Apologies To Maya Angelou)

The free cat leaps onto next-door's fence
and glides along till the fence just ends
and dips his paw in the garden pond
and dares to claim the goldfish.

But a cat that wails in the cupboard all night
can plan and plot until daylight
his exit is blocked and compromised
so he opens his throat to sing.

The caged cat sings with fearful yowl
of the things he wants and will have somehow
and his tune is heard by the wakened dead
for the caged cat sings of freedom.

The free cat thinks of only himself
and the mouse that runs on the kitchen shelf
and the fat birds waiting on a dawn-bright lawn
and he makes the world his own.

But the caged cat stands on fresh warm towels
his shadow shouts on a nightmare foul
his exit blocked and no one around
so he opens his throat to sing.

The caged cat sings with fearful yowl
of the things he wants and will have somehow
and his tune is heard by the wakened dead
for the caged cat sings of freedom.

Annie Hatton

Animal Antics

All alone, milk bottles stand in a line of three
Blackbird suddenly swoops upon them as nectar does with bee.
Looking into a crooked window can be seen a parrot
His antics brought the fun today as he retrieved a carrot.
Frivolous at a party when he miaows like many cats
A sailor brought him back, I'm told from the Horn of Africa.
And now he swings on a rope and sings, *I come from paprika*.
Such hilarious laughter at a party, you'll agree
Is better than church sermons when the hassocks bend the knee.
When dark shadows loom, magic has a chance
And ostriches run together to make a chariot dance.
They speed frantically at forty miles per hour
Such speed can be most helpful when caught in any shower.

Tom cabin

JoJo

I watched you at birth
a scrap of wet gold
entering the world
in the hay barn
on a spring day.

I mended your damaged leg
and so you became
part of our family
not a farm cat
like the others.

You shared our life
and enjoyed our holidays
and journeys up and down
the country in cars and on
ferries to islands.

You climbed mountains
and played in the snow
a spark of orange fur
shining in the whiteness
of the landscape.

You thought all visitors
came to see just you
and shared many a barbecue
and picnic
with friends and family.

Now, you are not here.
I miss your friendship
and the love you had
for everybody.
Sleep well, dear JoJo.

Judy Rochester

Just Good Friends

When Alan Mac visited
his good friend Jean,
he stood and enacted
the funniest thing I've seen.

Now Jean had a beagle -
Barney - long and fat,
who awaited Alan's visit
eagerly - drooling on the mat.

He eyed Alan as his hand
to his pocket crept,
extracting a thin package,
which he carefully unwrapped.

This was a sticky toffee bar,
which Barney watched for his cue,
when it was tossed in the air
he caught it, as was his due.

He bit it in eager anticipation
and drooled on the floor,
as he vainly tried to chew it,
with his toffee-locked jaw.

Alan chortled with amusement,
enjoying his harmless fun,
it certainly deterred Barney's barking
whenever he visited his home!

Suzanna Wilson

My Tiny Friend

Now, what can be said about Honey
And how she melted my heart?
Well, she was small and somewhat timid
But I loved her from the start.
And it didn't take long for Honey to see
That on me she could depend,
She looked to me for everything
And in return she was my friend.
As time went by her routine grew
And together each morning we'd dine,
She had her own bowl of cornflakes
But always preferred to share mine.
And after breakfast was over
She'd lick her paws and wash her face,
Then off to gather things for her bed
To her 'bits and bobs' bag she'd race.
I filled her bag with tiny toys
And paper balls that I'd made,
And each item was chosen with care
By Miss Honey before it was laid,
Her bed was now all plumped and fresh
And to her it looked so neat,
She could now lick jam for my finger
As her final morning treat.
Every day Honey's innocents
Would cheer me up and make me smile,
And even at my lowest times
Honey made my day worthwhile.
But science had given her cancer
And no matter how hard she tried,
Within weeks she could go no more
And my sweet tiny angel died.
There will always be an empty space
Where you and your home once sat,
I miss you so much honeysuckle
My precious little fancy rat.

Pauline Jones

Honey

A scared homeless terrier from Broome
Was saved by kind people from doom
From being put down
Now a new home has been found.
Before wandering alone on the streets
Looking for food or a kind face to greet
Hard sometimes to find a safe haven at night
Away from harm that was her plight
Of wire cages, of stranger's hands
Making so many, many demands
A good life now such a contrast
Expressive brown eyes melted our heart
Fell in love with her right from the start
Now we had our girl we could gloat
Cute as a button with her scruffy coat
We responded and made that connection
All she ever wanted was love and affection
Unconditional love, what more could we ask
In time bad memories will fade of her past
Her nature is kind but wary of strangers
Till she gets to know them, then there's no danger
We felt it was time for a new little pup
To fill in the void and cheer us right up
So wonderful to give Honey a new home
With her family she's now safe to roam
Laughter, fun times to be had
To keep us young sure won't be too bad
So, Honey, we're so thankful you came into our life
To stay with us forever, to give us new life.

Karen Holm

My Little Dog

Sloppy kisses on my bed,
'You're not allowed up here,' I said,
She stared at me with angled head
Did my little dog.

Postman comes and *rat-a-tat-tat,*
Delivered letters hit the mat,
She's up, she's off, she's there and back,
Is my little dog.

The park in spring, just dog and ball,
Wears Nature's gown and most of all
Becomes the Heaven so broad. so tall,
Of my little dog.

The love, the trust that I have found,
I bought all this for forty pound,
No Potters field, no Judas ground,
Just my little dog.

Joyce C Langlands

Just The otter Day

Otter munching in the river
glinting in the sun
light ripples to the shore
diving deep for prey
crayfish silver bubbles
persisting on the surface
floating out to sea
body drifting in the flow
curling, circling, crunching
underneath the by-pass
arching back taking the plunge
tail flipping into the air
trailing round behind
out there in the middle of the day
two too hungry cubs to feed
heading back upstream
flashes of silver behind
log come alive
posing for my camera eye
cheesy grin upon the chin
two folk watch with binocs
entranced on the opposite bank
making not for the marsh channel
but a holt close by my side
tide and time
well and truly
in.

P Hawkes

Nothing But A Hound Dog

Through the bars, I whispered, 'Will this work out?'
You gazed up at me.
Ten other dogs barked their heads off.
Unanswered, I had my doubts.
Fees paid, testicles drained,
You sprang to our yard and home,
Burying fast your new bone.
O'erwhelmed by men's needs,
I feared you'd want blow jobs,
Beer, a good listener.
Wide was blown my anxious mind!
We rambled in parks,
Snow-galloped, prairie-sniffed, aspen-hiked,
Fearless, roamed through dark alleys,
Angry 'hoods no woman should go,
Yet with you I strode dauntless
And strangers passed.
Now twelve, legs shot, death so close,
Still your tail wags as you totter about.
We gaze at each other,
'Will this work out?'

Lara Loory

Loss

Tiny-clawed pepper-pot cat,
you came from behind the fridge
hoping for food; swept into my hands,
small as a palm, and trembling.
A birthday surprise for my love:

hands held out, eyes closed -
for chocolate? A book? No -
the lightness of twenty pin-prick claws
- so small we named you Nutmeg.

Stipple-furred feral, you grew and played
in the sand, pranced along the shoreline,
bristled at the waves; sea cat,
storm cat; sand-hopper island cat -
weather-worn cat.

And then you didn't come;
we waited, listened at night
for the cat flap, paws
and purr. You

are somewhere
coiled and still, rocked
in a meadow, with grasses
and flowers, and the heat of the sun
still warms your fur.

Miriam Darlington

My old Dog

My old dog practises death
in her snug sleeping basket
Her breathing now so shallow
breast barely rising at all
Eyes, half closed, stare unseeing
into the deepest abyss

She wasn't always like this -
life once lifted her aloft
She sang songs of silliness
playful yaps of deep delight
Tiny treats set tail wagging
always willing for a walk

Old age crept up too quickly
catching us both unaware
So, now she practises death
on her soft grey lambswool rug
Her basket in the corner
brimful of dog - for now

And I wonder - as you do
projecting onto myself
Will I practise my death too
when my time starts to come around?
Is it something we all do
if we are granted the time?

Lin Edwards

The Confession of A Cat

Like a pile of compressed fog
caught on a twig at the mountain waist
the cat hunches on the sofa's shoulder
where I see the whole house of life
genetically domesticated behind the doors
that most hateful human invention

yes, I am a bimental being
as my feline friend has revealed
I can readily detect the moods
of my human family members
often switching my personality
with my drifting kittenhood
as I tease or avoid them behind doors
who know I enjoy solitary stalking
and respect my rented privacy
but none of them was born in the year of my day
since my ancestor was cheated shamefully
out of a ridiculous race in Chinese zodiac

the inside doors are ajar or unlocked
but the one facing the free spirits of nature
is always tightly closed, separating me
from my other self born to prefer
to stroll in the wild than sit in the house
once I sneak out of the threshold
I will never give a backward glance
yet I will keep my grooming habit
by using my long tongue to clean the dirtiest
and most private parts of my authentic being
somewhere in the wildness.

Changming Yuan

My Dog, Penny

I have a little dog
As cheeky as can be
She loves her walks and her toys
I know she loves me.
Her name is Penny
She chases all the cats out of my garden
She loves her little cuddles
I love her a lot.
She is my pal and comforter
She cuddles up beside me when I go to bed
Quiet now, she is sleeping
And having lovely dreams.
Then she wakes and kisses me
In her funny way
So we are beginning
Another happy day.

Anna R Spinks

Sammie

We had never really liked cats
My husband Bill and I
We loved our dog, perhaps too much -
Why did he have to die?

Then Sammie came into our life
His mum had gone away
And left him with a cat-sitter
But Sammie would not stay.

He liked the look of our backyard -
Preferred it to his own
'I think I'll stay with them for now,
Better than being alone.'

His 'mum' returned a few weeks on
Saw Sammie in the street
Then he walked in through our open door
Straight to his favourite seat.

Sammie's mum knocked on our front door
'Could he become your cat?
For I'm unable to take him
When I move to my high-rise flat.'

We've become adoptive parents
To a cat whose needs are few
He's made us into cat lovers now
It's almost as though he knew.

The moral of this little tale
Is clear to one and all -
A cat will *make* you love him
Just as soon as he comes to call.

Margaret Jones

What A Pig

Born in a house which we call a sty
With a bed of straw on which to lie
Small, round and pink with some very coarse hair
A new piglet so sweet with never a care.

There are sizes and colours of every hue
Black, black and white, spotted ones too
Long, long backs with a tail short and curly
Large ears, large snout, all 'hurly burly'!

They snuffle and oink as they rout round their bed
Contented and happy as long as well fed
They eat meal and water made to a 'slurry'
Which they slurp and they slurp, in a terrible hurry.

No manners, no need, it's first come, first served
A creature of habit it's really absurd
It's really a pleasure to watch all their antics
I love them - their ways - and their actions so frantic.

If I could choose an extra special pet
I would ask for a piglet - the one I would get
Would be small, round and spotted with patches of brown
The very best pet in the whole of our town.

Patricia Marland

Jaxson Pup

My mum was a Jack Russell,
My dad a Patterdale,
My adopted mum is very nice,
And I don't mean to be naughty,
Chasing anything that moves
And coming in all dirty.
It's in my genes you see,
So I find it very hard,
To ignore those furry balls of fluff,
That run around the yard.

Bunnies are my favourite,
I can see them at fifty yards,
Mum thinks I haven't seen them,
But I've got them in my sights.
When I get my chance I will have a go
And run with all my might.

I've got my eyes on those woolly things,
With funny little feet,
They stand about just chewing,
Then they start to move and bleat.
I would love to have a go at one,
But I know that, one thing is for sure,
Mum's farmer friend would be after me
And I would be no more.

So I'm going to be a good boy
And do as I am told,
I will even leave the cat alone,
I know it's her home too
And she keeps me warm at night,
When I'm missing Dad and you.

Elizabeth Turner

I'm Just A Little Puppy

(By Wag, the dog, aged 7 months)

I loved my rubber chicken;
I liked it when it squeaked,
But then I chewed its beak off
And both its floppy feet.
Sometimes we play at tug and chase
And a game of fetch and drop,
But once I got a telling off
For swallowing a sock.

I like it in the garden,
There's more for me to do,
With sticks and pegs
And plants and wasps,
There's lots for me to chew.
I can dribble, I can drool,
I can trump and snore,
And once I had a gongle
That dangled to the floor.

I sit and stay,
Go walks and play,
I can even do a trick,
But I'm just a little puppy
And I tire quite a bit.
Lunchtime is the best time,
With a bowl of what I like
And then it's time to sleep it off,
Wow - this is the life.

Ian Shipley

Mandinka Ray

The richest wine under hand as
Silk drapes across his muscle.
The sun draws fire,
Yet so gentle is he.
White daggers
On his brave face and still
He will leave no mark on me.
A beast of beauty
Admired by all,
Running, jumping, stands bold and tall.
Majestic in his flight
Pounding down on his land.
Such loyalty, such trust.
A crown of Crufts
He holds to his name,
At home he is but Roo.
A friend, a charming face
And love to come back to.

Elana Rose

Cuthbert My Cat

Cuthbert my cat was afraid he'd get fat
He decided to go on a diet
He's given up cream and chicken supreme
He won't even eat fish if I fry it.

He'll eat salad and greens or tender green beans
But he won't eat fat pork if I buy it
His figure's much neater, since he's been on Ryvita
But if I offered him chips he would riot.

It's just dawned upon us, why this feline Adonis
Is concerned what he eats for his dinner
There's a marmalade queen at number sixteen
And our Cuthbert's determined to win her!

Gerry Boxall

Untitled

Horses like people,
Just love to go neigh,
'Cause when problems arise,
It's so easy to say.
They don't try to face it,
They run, hide, or play
And never use horse sense
To chase it away.

Jay Berkowitz

our Bitch, Lucy

Our bitch was poodle Lucy
And we loved her.
After twelve years of buffooneries
Hair fell from her back, left it bald.
Scabious warts with scaly scurf, popped up;
Misty, grey-blue cataracts clouded Lucy's vision;
Bowels became incontinent, her stench was everywhere -
And we loved on
But when she died it was an act of mercy.

Matthew Timms

My Cat

My cat is glaring,
I glare unconsciously
Oh dear, he has claws . . .

Emma Jane Foster

Lilly The Jack Russell

Lilly is a terrier, not very big in height
But would not shame herself if engaged in a fight
Lilly's owners thought the world of her, spoiling her no end
Lilly did not understand all the attention, she didn't comprehend
Lilly had many admirers when taking her daily walk
People would stop and pass the time of day and talk
There was more chance of the local vicar being unfrocked
Than Lilly suffering the humiliation of having her tail docked
Lilly's bodily physique was rippling with sinuous muscle
Not always apparent in a diminutive Jack Russell
She learned to sit and fetch on command
To seek out and retrieve objects to hand
Lilly had a life of contentment in a comfortable home
And liked nothing more than to gnaw on a big, juicy bone.

Francis Rawlinson

Bilton's Carol

(To be sung to the tune of 'Away in a Manger')

Shut up in a stable, no comfy, warm bed,
The little dog Bilton laid down his wool' head.
The swallows were nesting, but now they have flown,
And little dog Bilton is all on his own.

The 'satians are barking, and Bilton, next door,
That little dog Bilton can't sleep on the floor.
I love you, dear Bilton, forgive me I pray,
If I have to leave you th' occasional day.

Jo Brookes

Jonesy

I've acquired a lodger, now it's his home,
Suddenly appearing, scraggy and alone,
He comes and he goes, never a by-your-leave,
Yet we've become good pals, would you believe?

He's Jonesy, the cat, a mate, or maybe lost son.
We meet at the door, he looks up and treads on.
An independent guy, he keeps himself to just him,
Then disappears, gone, somewhere on a whim.
Cruises back home, when he's good and ready,
Proud and stately, tail a-swish, ever steady.

He purrs, rubs himself against my legs and feet,
He's the only one that loves them, his and my treat.
Listens to my tales of woe, my moans and groans,
He's my conscience, my confessor, the Rev Mr Jones.
I think he's in love, his trysts are very mysterious,
He appears in the morning, always looking imperious.

So proud and good-looking, he thinks he's the bee's knee,
I believe he's my alter ego, he's so very much like me!

George Carrick

Bunny's Lot

I'm shut in this shed,
Out of sight, out of mind?
Please don't just leave me alone
In a dark, damp hutch.
In summer, it gets so hot in this shed,
Couldn't you just open the door?
I just want to lie in the cool, sweet grass,
Feel the warm sun.

I have thoughts and I have feelings too,
I haven't got anything to look at
And I haven't got anything to do.
How would you feel, locked in one room
Day and night, night and day?
That's not the way I want to live my life.

Please let me out in my run.
I don't want to be just left for dead.
So, please give me some kind of quality of life,
I am, after all,
Supposed to be your friend and your pet.
Perhaps you should just let me go
To someone who cares?

You're not really much of an owner,
Or should that be keeper,
For you don't own my soul.
I know you're always busy,
But I won't take up much of your time.
You asked *me* to live here, remember?
Please do your best,
For your best is what I deserve,
No less.
Don't let my life be lived in vain.
It's not too late, I'm still here,
Patiently waiting, here in this shed.
Maybe one day you will start to love and to care?
Why didn't you just buy a stuffed toy instead?
Please don't just leave me in this shed.

N J Brocks

For Billie

Oh, small brown dog
the fear I saw in your huge eyes
as you peered out at me
from within your cold, dirty prison cell
two paws placed on a ledge
your nose pressed through the bars of your confinement.
Oh, small brown dog
did I choose you
or did you choose me?

Now, medium-sized brown dog
your paws are growing larger, that I can see
my slippers lying in tatters
all daily routines are beginning to change for me
what did I release from that prison?
Oh, medium-sized brown dog
did I choose you
or did you choose me?

Ooh! Very large and boisterous brown dog
who chases my poor cats from room to room
upturns and chews things when left on her own
eats everything and anything
that isn't nailed to the ceiling
your paws are growing *larger!* brown dog.

But wait!
You run, play and give me endless hours of fun
would never hurt me
or make promises that you couldn't possibly hope to keep
invade my private space when I want to be alone
then irritate and bore me.
Oh *what a dog!* brown dog
whether you chose me
or I chose you
Welcome... *my Billie.*

Irene Reddish

Animal Antics

We'd gone to see what the dealer had got
And oh! they were a motley lot.
My grandson said, 'That donkey will do.
Can I call him 'Kangaroo'?'

Now that was eighteen years ago
But *tempus fugit* as you know.
Yet looking back I must confess
His life has been a great success.

Along with Pearly King and Queen
In London he has often been.
Outside Buck Palace he will stand
And listen to the marching band.

One day he had an interview
With Princess Alexandra too.

At Christmas he'll go door to door
Delivering goodies to the poor.
With harness polished, looking smart
He pulls a little governess cart.

He'll join a team of three or four
To 'log pull' from the forest floor.

But take him to a donkey show
And he'll say, 'No, oh no, no, no!'
Boring, boring, boring,
So he stands there - snoring.

But he asks for so little and gives me so much
So always let sympathy dwell in my touch.

Herdis Churchill

Vincent

This little Yorkie treasure
Was the inspiration to my verse?
His picture gives such pleasure
Without a trouble barking curse
To the world he shows his painting
From his little make-believe mind
Another doggy Van Gogh
Would be very hard to find
With his satisfied expression
Vincent would have one believe
That his canvas work and brush strokes
Are really some things to achieve?

E L Hannam

The Devil's Nap

Silently he slumbers, all is as should be,
The paper's where we left it,
The cushion's undisturbed,
The only noise we hear, comes from the lone TV.

A twitch of paw and flick of ear,
The dream is slowly fading,
An eyelid flutters, he voluntarily mutters,
The Devil's reappeared.

Rested from his lengthy kip,
He seeks to cause great mischief,
Unsettling those present with one swift move, vulnerable, exposed,
He readies for the nip.

Four great plates of meat bear down,
Fetid breath hits your cheek,
Resistance now is futile, he knows that you are weak.
The mighty grail he holds aloft, the belt from your dressing gown.

Hannah Tyrrel

Kitty Cat

I love to prance around
My tail in the air.
I'm the king of the castle
The mistress of the realm.

I sip milk
From my golden bowl -
Miaowing for more.
But my secret is Jammy Dodgers
My paws in the biscuit tin.

How cute they say.
But I have a dark side
Mr Dog watch out!
My claws will skin you alive . . .

I crawl back into my basket
Until another beautiful day.
Kitty says goodnight!

Jagdeesh Sokhal

Jakus Maximus

Before you see him, you will hear him,
Barking away with all of his might,
A bundle of white joy bounding towards you,
To try to ignore him is not worth the fight.

The little tornado encompasses you,
And there he will stay until he is done,
If you dare move away from him, you gain a new shadow,
Like it or not, this little boy wants to have fun.

He has interpreted 'lay down' as meaning 'walk time',
As soon as these words are said, the fun begins,
Twenty spin circles later and a few barks for good measure,
Jake is ready for adventure and always wins.

Lead on, the little dog marches proudly,
To his favourite spot where we are bound,
He keeps a lookout for the usual suspects,
If he doesn't bother for them he will stand his ground.

You see this little man thinks he is up there with the big guys,
'Ten ton' some would describe him with a laugh,
But if you don't want his generous attention,
Be sure not to walk down the path!

His mischievousness makes him more loveable,
His good-tempered nature shines through and through,
He's the first to give you a kiss in the morning,
Until something else catches his eye, that is true.

It's amazing how much happiness one dog could bring,
I'm certain the postman would say otherwise,
His unique character is what makes us love him so,
You feel blessed when you look into those eyes.

Elizabeth Hawkins

Cat Flap

While walking in the local park
One bright and sunny day,
I noticed a large ginger cat
Pursuing lunchtime prey.

A flock of birds were unaware
Of danger close and near,
They continued pecking breadcrumbs,
Without a trace of fear.

Just as the cat prepared to pounce,
It leapt high off the ground,
Front paws flapping and jaw snapping,
It howled a screeching sound.

A hornet, wasp or bumblebee
Had launched a quick attack,
The birds flew off, the cat slunk off,
Without its tasty snack.

Brian M Wood

Buster's Story

My breeders wanted a working dog
And although I'm always willing
It's like you humans always say
I'm sixpence short of a shilling
I've ruined carpets, furniture and things
Been told many times I will have to go
So behaved myself for a week or two
Until tempers began to slow
My family are all wacky folk
Lots of parties, lots of fun
And I believe in human sayings
'If you can't beat them, join them'
Now here is me after a party
Looking a little worse for wear
But fat and full and tired
So it's sleep for me in the chair.

D Fryer

My Friend

I lost my special friend
After fourteen years together.
At the beginning of friendship
You think it lasts forever.

But, that's not so,
One day we all must die.
Now my heart is sad
And many tears I cry.

One day I will find
Another special friend,
And with their friendship
My falling tears will end.

J Brown

Como

My little dog
Eats like a hog
Sleeps all day
Just his way
Getting too fat
To chase that cat
No longer bold
He's getting old
The best pet
Anyone could ever get
All I know
I love him so
Had him since a pup
Been fun watching him grow up.

Frank Tonner

Our Cat, Fluff

Our cat, Fluff, doth rule the night
All ye rodents feel a-fright
Terror strikes in tooth and claw
Death shall come with furry paw.

Our cat, Fluff, doth love the moon
Morning cometh all too soon
Lo, a scratching of the mat
Enter in ye purring cat.

Now she lieth on the bed
A feline moggy born and bred
Purring loud the windows shake
Dreaming of a sirloin steak.

John Cook

Gorilla Warfare

Sid, an infant gorilla,
whose old man was a killer
and whose mam was as tough as a nut,
hoped he'd grow up as strong
as his idol, King Kong,
but, alas - there was always a but.

Sickly, not very tall,
hunchbacked, knock-kneed and small,
with a squint about which he was bitter,
he'd most likely have flourished
had he been better nourished,
not the runtiest runt of the litter.

He sent off for equipment -
a very large shipment -
to develop his forearms and chest.
His old man all too soon he
growled, 'Kid, you're just puny.
Try giving the dumb bells a rest.'

So, to combat his ills,
he tried vitamin pills,
herbal remedies taken with honey
spread on blackcurrant bun.
But his mother said, 'Son,
this is costing us oodles of money.'

Sidney took to his bed
where he constantly read.
He loved literature. Wouldn't you know it?
Came one magical night
when he started to write.
Now - though puny - he's also a poet.

Norman Bissett

The Fox

He was a magnificent creature standing there
Tail spread out in the midnight air.
His keening noise had woken me
From sleep, from a slumber
Peaceful and deep.

Poised and listening
Still as stone
In the middle of the pavement
All alone.

I stared out the window
And caught his eye.
In a moment he saw me
Then shot on by.

Up the road
As quick as a flash
A proud young fox
All in a dash.

But just for a moment
A second in time
We stood together making a pair,
Stood as one in the midnight air
With the rubbish all scattered to prove he was there.

Ruth Clarke

A Poem For A Parrot

He-she's an African grey parrot;
What we've got!
With a soft, pink tail and an inquisitive beak,
You laugh out loud when you hear him speak.
18 years old, you'd never guess
And turns his cage into a terrible mess.
We have tantrums and occasionally we bite,
But like to have a cuddle just before we say goodnight.
We bow our head 'cause we love a scratch
And a chocolate digestive - well! There's no match.
I fly quite well, though the house is quite small,
But I've got my freedom and have a ball.
Sitting on my perch, I can ring my bell
And when no one notices me, I give it hell!
My drinking bowl is really for water,
But when my mother changes it,
I have a bath, just like I ought to.
I'm Sam Parrot,
Lest you forget.

Kevin Hornby

Sasha

I have a dog called Sasha, she really is a card
What she does around the house, makes life very hard

She bites at the rubbish bag, over the floor it all goes
Then into the laundry basket, chewing some of our clothes

Cushions from the sofa, are pulled all round the room
We try hard to catch her, but she's off with a zoom

Over the fence she jumps, smashing flowers as she lands
Where's that Sasha gone now? I bet she's got some plans

Sasha's gone into the kitchen, pulled our joint down on the floor
Chewed up all the spuds and greens, then hopped it through the door

There's holes in all my slippers, Sasha's bed's a right old mess
Whatever will she think of next? I daren't begin to guess

Sasha comes in from the garden, up the passage she does traipse
With mud on her paws, she jumps up at the drapes

Then off up the stairs, I'd better follow just in case
Oh, she's chewing the soap, it's all over her face

Sasha lets out a whine, 'cause it gave her quite a scare
She didn't go much on this, but it's made her more aware

Sorrowfully she looks at me, with great big, saddened eyes
And I cannot be angry anymore, instead I just surmise

That Sasha's learnt her lesson now and keeps well out of trouble
She coughs, and burps, and hiccups out, a great big soapy bubble

I put her in her basket, she's had a very busy day
With all these impish goings on, I hope that's where she'll stay

Sasha's really a very big handful, I don't know how I cope
She'll go and have a nightmare now,
And get chased by a bar of soap.

Olive White

Bruno Was So Special

Bruno was Dawn's dog, before Simon came on the scene,
a true and loyal friend, by her side he had always been.
When Jaz was little, he'd protect and keep them from harm,
pricking his ears up and barking, he was better than any alarm.
As soon as he got to know you, he would meet you at the door,
he liked you to make a fuss and he would give you his paw.
He'd always scrounge for food and would always be your mate,
eating leftover food, from your dinner plate.
Everybody loved him, Bob and Jess too, but sometimes
he was naughty, jumping over the gate to the loo.
The day came when he could go no further, he was tired and
needed a rest, now he is in doggy heaven, playing with other pets.
There will always be a special place in their hearts, because they
loved him so, but his spirit will be around, wherever they may go.
I hope he approves of Harry, who needed a special home,
who knows, they might be together, when Bruno's spirit roams.

S Bentley

Quizzical Gazing

I needed a quiet moment.
I needed thoughtful peace,
somewhere between winter and spring.
Warm enough to sit by an open door
wrapped around in a blanket;
Eyes closed and breathing deeply,
I stayed in my silence.
To listen and feel the air on my skin;
my body comfortable inside the warmth
of the blanket, settled deep in my chair,
everything a silent serenity.
A fleet movement close by -
I opened my eyes and looked
into the quizzical gaze of a fox;
stock still at the open door.
Neither of us moved or breathed
for what seemed an eternity.

Margaret Swan

How Weird!

Imagine how weird the world would be
If kangaroos swam in the sea
If wiggly worms had feathers
Or an octopus lived in a tree

Imagine how weird the world would be
If fish were furry, like cats
If a rabbit had an elephant's trunk
Or if bears hung around, like bats

Imagine how weird the world would be
If the sun shone green in the sky
If the sea was red and grass was blue
Or if pigs had wings and could fly

If this world as we know it
Suddenly disappeared
And everything came back jumbled up
Imagine... how weird!

Kath Cooley

To Jim

I didn't want to like you, young Jim
Golden retriever with soulful eyes.
I thought this affection's a passing whim,
How you took me by surprise.

I bade you go home to your master,
But you stood - unmoved - by my side.
I guessed all would end in disaster,
Inner warnings of woe-betide.

Yet you pawed away at this heart of stone,
Until, of course, I caved in.
It's my 'patch' now, where you bury a bone,
On Richard's face? A big grin!

Beryl Mapperley

My Pet

I have a strange and freaky pet
it weighs about a pound
It lives inside a fish tank
walking slowly round and round.
The tank is dry but has some soil
and lots of veg and fruit
My little pet enjoys the lot
though how I can't compute.
Now let's describe my little pet
without a dance and song
Her single foot's three inches wide
her shell's six inches long.
Her mouth has twenty thousand teeth
but not a single nail
She 'walks' at just two feet per hour
and could hide in a pail.
So though a strange and freaky pet
she's not that very odd
As long as she's kept nice and warm
she's a happy gastropod.
But there are just two little words
you must never, never utter
Because she would be most upset
if you said 'garlic butter'.

D G W Garde

Walking The Dog

Me and my dog we walk most every day
And fancy that, a pub lies on our way
He gets a bag of crisps and I a beer
We carry on our walk, full of good cheer
Ah! there's another house of hospitality
I wink at him, he grins at me
As if to say, 'It wouldn't be a sin
If you and me should just pop in
I'll have a sausage roll, and you a drink or two.'
This walking's very good for you
Just to go rambling at a steady gait
The thing is, we both seem to put on weight
The wife is pleased, she says it keeps us fit
And we don't tell about the other bit!

Gordon Andrews

Most other Animals

stop still to do it.
Human beings chisel whole
rooms around it.
Cats dig up
flowers to do it.
Even dogs
settle to it
around their lamp posts.

But cows and birds
share a talent
to manage it moving.
Birds like to do it
on new paint and hairdos
and hats at weddings.
Sometimes they succeed
in aiming it right into
your coffee cup.
Cows haven't got
the knack yet.

Rosemary Benzing

Cat

The cat
Likes
Being with
Humans.
It's a man's
Best friend.
It can't
Stop following
You about
And driving
You round
The bend.
It lies here.
It lies there.
It's a new
Ornament, it
Lives in your chair.
It doesn't
Coordinate.
It might break
Something
Sooner or later.

Nicola Barnes

Tina

'Come and see Mum,' they said,
If she's there on Monday she'll be dead!
Wasn't a bit like the dog I'd planned,
I wanted something rather grand.

One eye pink, the other brown,
A Jack Russell by renown.
We took her home, she fitted in,
When first we left her it was a sin.

Nothing in its proper place,
Kitchen was a real disgrace.
Next time we went out,
Gave her room to move about,
Soon settled down, made us laugh,
Not cause a frown.

Took her to the beach one day,
A ball with us to run and play.
In the sea she would go,
Barked, swam, loved it so.

Wild Flower Lane she used to roam,
Sniffing all the way from home.
She'd sniff a ball out in the grass,
If one was there she would not pass.

Loved the stream and the mud,
Rolled in smells left by the stud.
Used to bark at the slightest sound,
We felt safe with her around.

Soon I became unwell and stressed,
Walking lost its former zest.
With surgery I got fit,
Now I'm walking quite a bit.
Became my dog, I thought she would,
My walks with her did me good.
Alas, she then became unwell,
Warts and waterworks gave her hell.
Hygiene reasons she had to go,
Sadly, we still miss her so.

I know one day we'll meet again
And her life was not in vain.
In a quiet and peaceful way,
This will take the grief away.

Olive Young

Hare Pie To Die For!

So you think it safe and that I don't care
If you burrow through my hedge into my garden fair
With those big limpid eyes holding all the world's fear
And your nervous reaction as you sense me draw near

Well, you're almost right Rabbit! You are not welcome there.
Though conscience dictates, your right to join in for a share
There is delight and surprise every time that we meet
Mine is the pleasure, yours the quick feet!

It's taken you a while to find my Shangri La
Thirty years have passed since I last saw your scare
From that awful disease man inflicted on your race
For your life of pain and struggle, we carry the disgrace.

These thoughts temper my reaction as through the garden you stray
But who's pushing his luck, look what's now in his way
My carrots; fresh lettuce he's made his first and favourite fare
Tolerance, compassion and fair play. Out the window and up in the air.

Our poor Lagomopha-Leporidae is now no longer to be seen anywhere
At the same time Fred's café in the High Street has an unusually rare country fare
Genus Lepus is now being served as the special
For those who can't tell their rabbit from hare!

Charles Keeble

A Friend That's Always There

When I feel alone and need a friend, you're there,
A friendly face, showing me that you care.
You sit close and listen to me, when nobody else will
And somehow you seem to understand exactly how I feel.
You are always there, when humans seem to fail,
A smiling face when I get home, sitting there wagging your tail.
A bond with a dog is one that will never break,
It's the best friendship that anyone could ever make.

Clare Beavis (15)

Deia

Hyperactive dog,
Leaping through the air,
Pursuing something thrown.

Eyes of orange-brown,
With rings of brighter gold,
And black and shiny hair.

Her tail wags again,
She looks down at the ball
Inquisitively, waiting.

Tom W Heenan

10 Years Anniversary Loss of My Dog, Gino

(1979 - 1997)

Yes, my dog, Gino
He was a wonderful dog
He was a dog everybody loved
He was always as good as gold
He was always treasured and loved
My dog, Gino, black and tan with a white mane
All my friends and family loved Gino
Family who didn't know him loved him too
Got footage of Gino on DVD I have
Many photographs of Gino I have
Gino Giovanni Flycatcher Hall
A marvellous, wonderful dog he was
He is now in Heaven with other members of my family
They look after him and are with him now
Born 13th September 1979
Died 31st July 1997
Lived 18 wonderful years
Yes Gino, well loved, met many stars and celebrities too
Yes Gino is always thought of
Still always remembered
Will never be forgotten
He was a wonderful, marvellous, fantastic dog
Always loved and treasured
Yes, my dog, Gino.

David J Hall

Happy Christmas Minou

Happy Christmas Minou Cat
And a great New Year!
We always wonder what you're at
To fill your days with cheer.
Whatever it may be, we know
You do not wander far;
Yet you've been known to fight the foe
And come home with a scar!
Your territory belongs to you
You defend it to the last,
Woe betide intruders who
Cannot run too fast!
But those you know, you love to meet,
With upturned tail and rubbing nose,
And purring; what a way to greet
Your friends, the ones *you* chose!
Happy Christmas, Minou Cat
And a great New Year!
Herewith we send a festive pat
With wishes warm and dear.

Christopher Head

Jim's Fish

I'm Jim, I'm six and my birthday is here.
The countdown is over, I've waited a year!
What gift will I get? A game or a toy?
A puzzle or book? Or a bike for a boy?
The excitement is rising as Mum leads me in
To the room in our house where the fun will begin.
She points to my present all pleased with herself,
And there it is... simply... a tank on a shelf.
Not a tank as in 'army', but a tank as in 'fish',
And my heart starts to sink; is this all there is?

I bite on my lip as tears well in my eyes.
A silly old goldfish... my 'birthday surprise'.
But I stare and move closer; we don't make a sound,
And I watch that small fish swimming round and around.
He spies me! He's startled! He darts to the side
Of the tank, but for him there is nowhere to hide.
Hang on! There's a skull and a ship on the bottom
Like a scene from an ocean of times now forgotten.
And my fish, he shoots down there and swims through the skull,
Then he scuttles around on the deck and the hull.

He is graceful and quick, coloured orange and black
With frills on his tail and stripes on his back.
He's a champion swimmer, a pirate, a shark
Who can flip through the water or lurk in the dark.
He peers at me now with his eyes round and wide,
Then he mouths a *'helloooo'* and this makes me smile.
I'm Jim and I'm six; I'm as pleased as can be
'Cause this really cool fish has been bought just for me!

Deborah Hamer

Rupert

My little dog called Rupert,
Is as cute as he can be;
The best dog in this whole wide world,
As anyone can see.

And if you were to meet him,
This handsome little guy;
I know that you would love him,
Just as much as Bill and I.

He likes to chase the squirrels,
Which can be a big disaster;
Rupert can run fast,
But squirrels move much faster.

Anyone who sees him,
Wants to stoop and pet and stroke;
Rupert, he just laps it up,
He would, cos he's a bloke.

Yes, he is a much loved pet,
Part of our family;
But when you ask, 'But who's the boss?'
I have to answer, 'He!'

Shirley Brooks

Dogstar Litter

(The Dogstar rises and sets with the sun between July 3rd and August 11th) *July 6th 2006*

Hairy-Mary
the gloating, nursing
German Shepherd with her first darling litter
didn't realise it would be like *this.*

At one day old all nine of them are
snuggling, nestling, tickling, squeaking,
cuddling, warming, sleeping and just so
wonderful.

August 6th 2006

At one month old the horde of them are
clawing, throbbing, gulping, yapping,
demanding, chewing, hurting and just so
awful.

Balding Mary
the frazzled, drained
Alsatian with her first dratted litter
had no idea it would be like *this.*

Francesca Bass

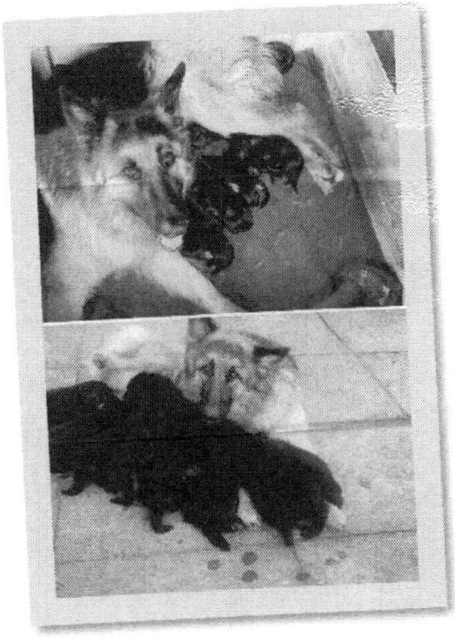

Lady And The Tramp

One of him and one of her, a wedded pair that really purr
Nibbling at each other's necks, always giving little pecks
Licking out their waxy ears, a sight to see when you are near
Grunts are groaned and wriggles done, these chairs are only made for one

Fur flying, ears dancing, paws high in the air
Tearing round the garden, I look on in despair
Then, big brown eyes and waggy tails come bounding up to me
We're only playing silly games, it's obvious, can't you see?

Matted fur and doggy hairs a-falling everywhere
Sharing beds and blankets, they are always very fair
She is such a floozy as she rolls into his face
He is such a rogue, resting his head on her rudest place

Mealtimes are for eating, they share each other's bowls
Then they fall asleep like snoring kindred souls
Then the wind starts blowing, so we rush out of the room
He's looking at his bottom as we laugh at all the fumes

Tatas is the highlight of any doggie's day
Watching them is funny in a silly kind of way
She is such a cutey and he is such a champ
Wedded bliss is perfect for the lady and the tramp.

Dawn Bennie

Skye

Ponderous and pouncy,
Bumptious and bouncy,
Huge soggy jaws,
Ginormous paws!
Droopy sad eyes and
A tail that sweeps the skies.

Powerful and playful,
Delightfully disobeyful!
Yards of skin to spare
And an arrogantish air!
A companion dear and true -
Yes, Skye my love, it's you!

Kim Thompson

Zeus

Zeus is an Akita,
A cute little pup.
He's smart and adorable
A real pick-me-up.
He loves to play.
His favourite toy is his teddy.
If we want to go for walks,
Zeus is always ready.
He's a real playmate
For our other dog,
But when it comes to food,
Zeus is a hog!
It's more than a friendship
Zeus and I share,
Whenever I need him,
Zeus will be there.
With his funny expressions,
He's a loveable hound,
I just can't imagine my life
Without Zeus being around.

Patricia Heard

Mission Impawsible

Late at night when the ceiling's dark
When the moon casts shadows on his favourite park
Arnie climbs the stairs to bed
To find a place to rest his head
With squeaky 'Rex' dragged up each stair
To keep away from the cat's stark glare
His wicker basket is cold and scratchy
With bits of twig that are chewed and tatty
He lies there, still - till they're sound asleep
When the house is still and the alarm goes bleep.
A paw stretches out, finding the carpet
He moved with precision, seeing his target
Scaling the floor, flat on his side
He reaches the bed and pauses aside
Have they noticed? He'll wait for a while
No sound or movement, so a paw, for a trial
Raises and lands on the side of the sheet
Pauses a second to be discreet
Still no shouts to go back to his corner
So another paw advances just like the former
Two big brown eyes peer and teeter
He springs on the bed with the speed of a cheetah
He's under the covers and snuggles in tight
He moves up close but the pillow's in sight
A sneaky roll from his back to his side
A shake of the tail, a slide and a glide
His goal is reached - the final frontier
Head in the pillow, duvet up to his ear
Flat on his back snoring with ease
I'll worry tomorrow about their fleas!

Leanne Flood

Herbivorous Carnivorous

Dinner's ready. No, that's mine. Get your nose off my plate,
Yours will be along in a minute if you'll only wait.
Yes, you can sit on my lap but keep control of that tail,
I don't want hairs grouping in my gravy or carpeting my kale.
You won't like it, best stick with your Felix and jellied delights,
Get down, I cannot stomach another of these foolish food fights.
I'm a vegetarian for goodness sake;
I don't eat pork and I don't eat fish
So will you please get down and investigate your own dish.
Nose out, paws up, step away from those peas,
Get down off the table will you please?
Mind the oven! The ring's hot, I've warned you before.
Paws off! You shouldn't like my cooking, you're a carnivore!
Really this behaviour is out of order, quite absurd,
You should be out in the garden stalking a bird.
It's not normal you know for a cat to crave a bean or sprout,
Your fundamentalist feline friends might laugh if word got out.
Paws off the table, I'm warning you! Oh, don't look at me like that,
There is no such thing as a herbivorous cat.

Andrea Mitchell

Lost

Where's me dog? Where's me dog?
He's got himself lost
in the snow and the fog.

I look in the yard and under the car,
on a night like this
he can't have gone far.

I check the stables but he's not there.
Oh where can he be?
Oh where? Oh where?

I call his name out loud and shout
for him to come back,
but he's nowhere about.

I tramp the fields and search the wood,
I know he'd come back
if only he could!

As tears stream down my face
the fear of not knowing,
sets my heart a-race.

I take my car and drive down the lane,
peeping the horn
and calling his name.

When I get home, he's still not found
so I shout him again,
but still not a sound.
I walk down to the pond and along the stream,
then wait for a while,
but he's nowhere to be seen.

Back to the house up the steps I slog,
I open the door
and there's me dog.

Charlotte A K Bailey

Timmy

A ball of fluff was Timmy
When first he came my way
And settled in my garden
Ten years ago today.
He seemed quite lost and frightened
Ran quickly out of sight
When I laid out a saucer
Of milk for him that night.

Next morning when I opened
The door, what did I see?
A little ball of fluff sitting
Staring up at me.
A little yawn, a little miaow
Then quickly as a flash
That tiny little kitten
Into the kitchen dashed.

I really meant to put him out
But as I turned around
He scampered right up to my feet
And made a purring sound.
His purring grew much louder
As I gave his head a pat
Then with a yawn he stretched himself
And settled on the mat.

M S Bradley

Podgy Paws

Podgy Paws has a demanding appetite,
For rawhide, tripe and affection.
A picture-postcard of loyalty,
He'll protect me.
I'll walk and feed him
He'll remind me when it's four o'clock,
With a barked request for dinner.
He'll tell me when it's walking time,
A lead between his teeth,
Not the most subtle hint.
And when I return home
After a long day out,
He'll remind with a wag of his tail
Just how much I'm loved.

Stacey Cavanagh

My Saddleback Pig

I adore my saddleback pig,
She just loves to root and dig,
With her wrinkled, short fat snout,
She loves the mud, there is no doubt!

Enjoying a stiff brush and pat,
Which in turn wobbles her fat!
Her curly tail wags with glee,
So happy she is, I do agree.

The nosh is placed in her trough,
All the food she loves to scoff.
Sleeping through the rainy day,
Snuggled in her bed of hay.

I can hear her squeal and grunt,
Greetings with a powerful shunt,
Her nose is muddy, moist and wet,
But she's a gorgeous loving pet.

With great big floppy ears,
From underneath she peers.
She shows me so much love,
By giving me a nuzzling shove!

Louise Tunnard

Skye

You'll find the bitch at the 'Townhouse Bar' most nights -
always in a fur coat, thin-legged, red choker, white pop socks.
A brazen hussy, she sits in a curl of smoke
listening intently to every drop of idle chat
enjoying the admiring stares of those who know her well
and those who don't.

Dark, soulful eyes arrest all who cross her path
she's used to jibes about her name
and doesn't blink when it's suggested she can be hired
for thirty pounds a month
or nine, sport only?

Children can be frightened of her at first, but soon realise
despite her scowl, she is as harmless as a summer breeze.
She prefers the company of men, enjoys the banter
and shamelessly, the drunken hands
that openly caress her legs and chest.

It's no secret, to those who know her well
her favours are for free - she doesn't come easily
only to the trusted few, if you're in luck
and for a few pork scratchings
she'll put her legs around your neck, pant, lick your face.

In her last life, maybe a hooker of some consequence
though some might disagree?
In this life a human soul entrapped within a boxer dog
and in the canine world, a creature
of the *highest pedigree!*

John Clark

Louie

With soft, fluffy, moulting fur
Runs away
From the creature that purrs.
Ticking of his claws on tile
Lazy eyes
That glow with a smile.
Wiggling toes, he will greet
Breathing warmth
Lies beneath my feet.
When it's time for me to leave
Grab my coat
He sniffs at the sleeve.
Scuffles up onto his feet
Runs ahead
At the door we meet.
Glances up to say bye-bye.
Could it be . . .
I saw a tear in his eye?

Joanna Muscat

Jennie, A Tortoiseshell Cat

We arrived at a pet shop in Surrey
My brother and sisters and me,
So soft, appealing and fluffy,
Unsure what our future would be.

One by one the siblings were bought
And I was left on my own,
A loving owner was my only thought -
Won't someone please take me home?

Two pounds fifty was all that I cost,
Not much for a kitten in need;
Alone, so frightened and utterly lost
In a world that seemed hopeless indeed.

In just a few days a lady came by,
She definitely wanted a kitten,
She lifted me out and held me up high,
Oh! Surely she had to be smitten.

She didn't take long to make up her mind
To buy this poor little waif,
I felt she'd be good, I knew she'd be kind,
So quickly the money she gave.

And now I'm as happy as happy could be,
I've so many places to roam,
With very good food and fish from the sea,
There's nothing quite like a good home.

Ever so quickly the years have gone
And now I'm a pensioner cat;
I sit in the garden and laze in the sun
And dream of catching a rat!

Maureen Alexander

Memories of Sasha

(In loving memory of my dog, Sasha)

M y dog, Sasha, closed her eyes and went to sleep
E ventually she woke and was in Heaven
M y Sasha was a good age of eleven
O h, I cried and cried when she died
R emembering her is easy
I loved her so much, I didn't want her to go
E ven though she's gone away
S he walks beside me every day

O h, how I miss her
F orever in my heart

S he will always stay
A ngels took her and it was such a sad day
S till always protecting me
H ow I wish I could see her one last time
A ll my love, my dear dog, Sasha, I wrote this rhyme just for you.

Stephanie owers (11)

My Friend, Mr Tiggs

(My cat)

I have a friend, he comes running to greet me
On my arrival home.
He rubs himself around my ankles
When I walk in the house.
At mealtimes my friend likes to sample
What's on the menu.
Often this can be today's special.
Often a bit of something I am eating.

When I settle to watch TV
My friend jumps up on my lap.
Then needs himself
Until he has found comfort.
He will then fall asleep on my lap
Wagging his tail.

When out in the garden
My friend follows me.
In the summer when sitting on the patio
Drinking a welcome cup of coffee
Lost in the pages of a good book

My friend sits by my side
Taking in the sun.
Then at night while I sleep
My friend lies by my feet.

If he feels like a night stroll
He will wake me
To open the door.
On his return
He strokes the glass
With his paws
Then miaows
To let me know
He is home.
My friend is called Tigger.
My furry friend.

Jane Coulston

our Alarm

Please, if you're a burglar
I have something to tell
Stay away from my house
As our alarm works very well

It might protect my neighbours too
They seem to think it will
As it can detect their every movement
With its superlative skill

Our alarm it is quite different
You see, it has a bark
A long black tail, great white teeth
And works mainly after dark

The slightest sound and out she goes
With hackles top to toe
And the deepest bark I've ever heard
Where it comes from, I don't know

Sometimes when we go to check
We find there's nothing there
But Misty seems to think there was
And we cannot break her stare

Her senses stay on full alert
Until she's satisfied
Then she'll give a final warning bark
And saunter back inside

Who needs a proper house alarm
When one with teeth works fine?
So please steer clear of my house
Or you might just trigger mine.

Julie Preston

Horny Herbert - The Saucy Swine

I've heard a most amusing tale
About a boar that could not fail
To propagate his porcine seed
With procreation guaranteed.

But this was not the time or place
For frisky porkers to embrace.
There simply was no rhyme or reason
For it was not the mating season.

Some say it was unseasonal heat
That made this pig perform the feat
Of charging through the sturdy fence
To end his sexual abstinence.

For grunting on the other side
A sow called Fifi he espied.
She looked so tempting he could not
Restrain himself, no matter what.

This titillating quadruped
Had teased him till he'd lost his head.
His raging hormones caused such stress
He broke the rules of politesse.

Two mouths met in an ardent kiss,
A prelude to a state of bliss.
Two lovers lost in amorous play
Conjoined with pleasure on the hay.

When squealing piglets filled the sty,
Horny Herbert could not deny
Paternity, for he had done
The deed in front of everyone.
He has so much testosterone
He cannot leave the sows alone,
But Fifi's favourite by a mile -
That's why she always wears a smile.

Celia G Thomas

In My Pocket

In my pocket
Plastic bags
Small change
And dog biscuits

These are the tools
We use to survive
No, I'm not homeless
But a dog owner!

And my dog
Is very demanding
He relies on me for walks
He relies on me for treats

He relies on me for love
And the feeling is mutual.

Barbara Tozer

Sunshine (My Racing Greyhound Girl)

My faithful friend you always are
of past, present and much more,
your beauty fills me with pride,
slender golden form glowing in the sun,
dark, honest eyes open wide
full of trust and purity,
they know the secrets of my soul,
yet, do I know your heart at all?
Remember the joy and glory,
those summer days on the racing track
where you left them all behind
and drank champagne from your silver cup
now we're both getting old and slow,
I cherish each moment we still have
to make good for the time
I ignored and forgot you,
too blind to see what you came to teach.
Let me take you once more today
to run with me along the beach,
watch your elegant stride,
carry you with the wind again
pure poetry in motion
when you chase seagulls dancing on the waves.

Sybille Sydney Krivenko

Dead Ringer

Sam
Jumps like a springbok,
Purrs like a cat,
Growls like a lion,
Well fancy that.

He joins in conversations,
Then grunts just like a hog.
Our collie, German Shepherd cross
Is such a clever dog.

Joyce Walker

Tasha

There she lay, as always, at the foot of the stairs,
Waiting to greet us at the start of another day.
We called her name: 'Tasha, Tasha!'
No bright eyes shone up in answer to our call;
No wagging tail full of the joyful energy of morning.
There she lay, peaceful in the solitude of sleep,
Never more to greet her human friends
Who'd cared for her and loved her all her days.
Eleven years and more she'd shared our home.
She was always there . . .
To guard the house while we were away,
To greet us jubilantly on our return,
To walk with us, and play with us,
Always our faithful companion and friend.
How much we miss her!
We still watch for her at every turn,
Expect to see her in her favourite haunts,
Look at the foot of the stairs each morning,
Await her welcoming bark and wagging tail,
When we come home at the end of each day.
Her toys have all been sadly stored,
Her collar and lead, her dish for food . . .
All put away, perhaps to be used
By another faithful companion one day.
Till then, all we have are memories,
Happy memories of this canine 'child'
Who shared our home, our love, our lives,
Never to be forgotten.

Margaret Worsley

Goodbye Sultan

(on losing my 14-year-old cocker spaniel)

The fuchsia buds still bobble in the breeze - and everything is *almost* just the same.
The laveteria's filled with humming bees; and *yet,* we'll never more call out his name.

The ghosts of summers past will haunt me now - that flash of 'Kipper' playing on the lawn
His fourteen summers banked in memory, and I am left alone to feel forlorn.

'Each time we say 'goodbye', we die a little' - yet his life was just as happy as could be
And there'll be summers new I can enjoy. The one big difference:
Now, there's only *me.*

Hannah Yates

Three-Legged Nina

Three-legged Nina, rotund little tabby,
She's nearly always found
Inside her igloo or on a chair
(If not too high to reach up there)
But rarely running around.

It's not that she can't run at all,
She's just a lazy cat
Who likes to creep
Where she can sleep
And that, says she, is that!

At one time she was grumpy,
A firebrand in the making,
She would scratch and bite
And pick a fight
And leave us all a-shaking.

Several years on and alone with me
She's calmer, more reposed
And if gently stroked,
Not kicked or poked,
She'll respond with a purr, eyes closed.

Three-legged tabby, our Nina,
Her coat now has silky shine,
She pats with claws *in,*
Sometimes seems to grin
That *she* owns me and mine!

She's a 'twelve-hour' little lady
With an appetite grotesque
And would eat all day
If she had her own way
And forget any arabesque.
For her love, of course, is cupboard love,
She's always ahead of time
By waking me far too early
And making me feel quite surly
Before my clock will chime;

She scratches at the bedclothes

Thinking I'll just give in,
Or play with my feet
As her way to greet
That feeding her 'late' is a sin!

Then three-legged Nina gets active
As she follows me up the stairs
And makes a big wish
That I'll *fill* all her dish
If she 'snuggles' my legs unawares!

Three-legged Nina, my hop-along tabby,
Can sometimes show affection
By a kiss on the nose
Though I think she knows
That's not the right direction.

Mostly she's just the quietest cat
Who likes to be left alone
Until time to eat
Then she's quick on three feet,
The fastest three-legger I've known!

Ann Voaden

Untitled

Your first six months were spent cramped in a cage
You grew up in size, but not in age,
We wished we'd have rescued you five months before,
So you wouldn't have hidden, in fear, in that drawer.

You shied from the light and from small open spaces,
Your new home was one of unfamiliar places,
To hold you we struggled, you fought to break free,
But we never gave up, because we could see,

That you needed our love if you were to thrive,
And behave like a cat we could see was alive.
It took years of slow progress with love and attention,
Though you never forgot the heartbreak of detention.

We watched you grow up, though, always just behind,
We showed you real love and you paid us in kind,
You lounged in the sunshine that you'd been denied
And to see you contented brought a warm glow inside.

Your black and white fur, always soft, had a shine,
And when something upset you, you'd just sit and whine.
But we knew that this meant you were finally you,
And our aim was accomplished, you stopped feeling blue.

And when last month you fell ill, no one could tell why,
We still never thought that, perhaps, you would die,
But your time here with us had now come to an end,
We just hope that you're happy, we miss you Mickey, our friend.

Phil Welham

Madam, The Wilful Cat

Please, don't look at me like that
I must remind you, Madam, that you are a cat.
I am the boss here; this is my house
I'm not a pushover and I'm not a mouse
For you to play with and have your way.
Now listen, Madam, to what I say!
You may look gorgeous but I know your lies,
That hypnotic purring, those soulful eyes.

You are sleek and sensuous, an elegant minx
But remember, Madam, I know all your tricks.
When you pay the bills for your room and board,
When you pay the vet of your own accord,
When you pay the piper, you can sing the song;
You may think I'll weaken but you are so wrong!
You may think you'll best me, make me your tool
But I tell you now, Madam, I won't play your fool.

Oh yes, I do love you, there's no doubt of that
But, I must remind you, Madam,
That you are a cat!

D M Griffiths

My Dog The Fluffy Robber

As the moon soaks me in its powerful rays,
I struggle out of bed, like I'm stuck in a maze.
I look out the window into the night,
I suck in my breath and make my chest go all tight.
Outside, out there prowling on the ground,
A big, furious thing that looks a bit like my hound.
Dripping from its mouth is silvery slobber,
Stealing from Mum's washing basket, just like a robber.
He looks up with a grin on his face,
Which would make him look quite cute if he wasn't a disgrace.
His fur is all wet from the rain above,
Oh, he may be naughty, but he knows he is loved.
But no, he insists,
A thousand ways I could list,
Saying what a nuisance he is,
Prancing, flouncing round the neighbour's dog, Liz.
He drives me in state,
Who knows why he is my best mate,
But despite all this, he isn't too bad,
But that doesn't change the fact that he's stark raving mad.

Lillian Walton

Pelham

Queen Pelham of Faithorn,
The first and the best,
Our history is scarred,
By slashes I'm blessed.

You got me through uni,
Dribbled over my work,
But love that you gave me,
Kept me with smirk.

My love for you ensured,
A meat-free diet for me,
Yet that diet of yours,
Many animals - no glee.

Cat heaven is snug with welcoming arms,
Food constant and lush, knowing your charms.
But I hope that you miss,
As I have done heaps,
No longer suffer my touch,
Please happy we sleep.

Sarah Faithorn

our Pussycat

When we got our pussycat
Her life was full of strife
As she didn't like her city home
And was used to country life

Our son was just delighted
As he took her from the car
To show his mum and sister
Our brand new family star

She settled in quite quickly
Though always found a place to 'hide'
Until she found her bearings
And was allowed to go outside

She is very independent
And likes to be herself
We all like to see her hunting
As she practises her stealth

She is a huge fan of feeding time
And always gets into such a state
She tells you most indignantly
If you happen to be late!

She's certainly never been a lap cat
Most autonomous and won't be led
Though her favourite winter night-time place
Is curled up cosy on our bed

She's a tremendous hunter
Catching mice of every size
Although my wife doesn't always appreciate
When she comes inside with her 'prize'
We've all grown to love her
Our white, low maintenance cat
And look forward to many, many years
Of her catching mice and rats.

Chris Leith

Rosie's Brother Could Be Feral

He'll hunt for mice from need, not sport,
then bask on garden shed shelves, to
sleep off his wild-meat meals;
surrounded by empty twine reels,
and jars that yield nut, bolt... screw.

Adroitly he steps round them as
if on a ballet dancer's pointes.
An AA badge might be dislodged,
to rearrange that quaint hodge-podge.
Pussies thrive on finding such joints.

Or else he wanders with his pals,
to chimneys they have known to smoke,
and huddle round them, twining tails -
gingers, torties, old queens and males
beneath the twilight's fusky cloak.

Gillian Fisher

Animals

My cats relax in every comfortable place,
However, should they spy a mouse,
They will certainly quicken their pace!

If only animals could talk
I guess my dogs would say . . .
'Isn't it time we went for a walk?
It is such a beautiful day.'

Our Highland cows contentedly graze
Beneath the warm sunshine
They also seem oblivious, when
Winter comes again and icicles
Hang from their heavy coats,
Every now and then.

Our heavy horses so gentle, considering their size,
Welcome carrots and titbits at least once a day
However, when the farrier arrives,
They'd rather he went away!

The love received from animals
Is second to none,
They are always so happy to see us
And to hopefully have some fun!

J C Igesund

Cat

Motorbike purr,
Paws outstretched,
You roll expectantly.
A servant summoned
I rub your willing belly,
Laughing with delight
As your scrunched face
Sings your pleasure.

Paul Howard

Free Spirit

Free spirit, feral born
Out at night, till dawn
Comes in for food and a loving word
She's caught a mouse and a bird
Her fur's so long, in need of a comb
All night long, she loves to roam

Free spirit, feral born
Out at night, till dawn
Then in the day, she tries to find a spot
To curl up in the sun, where it's hot
The higher the place, the better she will be
A rooftop, a window ledge, or even a tree

Free spirit, feral born
Out at night, till dawn
I love her dearly, with her owl-like ears
Her name is Fergie, I have had her for years
She has no collar, nor a bell
As she is a free spirit and you can tell.

Barbara Jackson

My Feline Friend

Our eyes
Meet
Over the wall
To have
Wordless
Conversations
Our eyes
Meet
When I raise
The ball up
For a reaction
Our eyes meet when she weaves a figure of
Eight around me for attention
A speechless language of love
Between a feline and a human
Our eyes meet
Behind her ears
A silent understanding
A knowing
When she purrs.

Marcia calame

The Wolves' Midnight Cry

The hungry wolves bay at the over-arching distant moon,
Aspiring to the brilliance of its lunar radiance,
The black stillness of the night enlightened
By the glaring lamp's vision.

The community of wolves stalk in search of prey,
Wearing the badge of harmonious unity,
Creating discord and chaos in the hunted.

The cool, ice-coloured eyes belying a smothering desire,
The clouds of hot, silvery breath contained,
In an anatomy of serene sophistry.

A passionate loyalty to the pack,
Is reflected in the betrayal of the prey,
Triumphant in the battle of wills.

The piercing, brightly coloured eyes,
Gaze with focused concentration,
Penetrating the soul of the viewed.

Hasan Erdogan

Bird Spotting With Bear

Sat on a flat-topped fence post
Watching out for birds
Your belly against your body size
Is probably two-thirds

Your fur looks nice and shiny
Against the morning sky
And for a moment, in my madness
You seem so cute and shy

But suddenly, from nowhere
Mr Blue Tit does appear
Hanging from the feeder
Without a sense of fear

He doesn't see you sitting there
So neat and looking nice
No wonder birds don't last round here
Not to mention any mice

I wish my furry friend here
Would fall asleep without delay
So Mrs Blue Tit's husband
Can return to nest today

But Bear's teeth begin to chatter
And she's poised in feline crouch
So will Mr Blue Tit make it
Or end up in her pouch?

I will leave you to consider
Who the likely winner is
But the cat is cleaning whiskers
And licking off her paws!

Charlie McInally

Animal Antics

Maggie is fun to be with
She's a Border Collie with a black and white face
Who loves to play with a big rubber ball
And knock it back to you with her lovely wet nose
She loves barking and going for walks
Smelling all the exciting things in the park
And chasing cats and squirrels who run up the trees
She's a man's best friend
Who comforts me when I am sad
And seems to understand me like my closest friend
She's made by our Creator
To bring us love
A furry friend to stroke with life from above
Children love to play with her in the garden
And shout with glee when she barks
She loves to sleep and eat doggie food
Never seems to worry or be sad
But cheers us up by her warm, friendly face.

D Cooke

Mad Cat

My cat has mad half hours
When she becomes a whirling blur of fur,
Careening around the garden.
Leaping, curving sideways
Vertical take-offs,
Horizontal spurts across the fence.
Then she becomes a fly,
Chases invisible prey,
Plays with unseen mice,
Circumnavigates the living room,
Leaps straight into the air.
And all the while she sings and laughs and bubbles,
Then she stops, becomes freeze-framed stillness,
Nothing moves;
She has become a china cat.

Off again,
Up the clothes pole, in my saddlebag,
On the fence, dustbin, window ledge,
Flat in the grass;
On hind legs chasing butterflies.

My cat has beautiful and mad half hours.

Carole Skidmore

Goodnight Waggie Maggie

We went on the Maggie walk today,
Christmas leaves rustling along the way
As we reached the pond
Where Maggie stood,
Knee-deep and snorkelling
As a Labrador should.

Last time we walked this way
Bluebells filled every wooded glade.
Now each drop of Christmas time is gold.
We want to collect it in a jar
And hoard it for the years ahead
When loved ones may be gone afar.

The oak trees spread leafless overhead
But all the tears for Maggie are shed.
The great sleep of winter
Folded gentle as a dove's wings
Round that great and giving heart.
As we stroked her loving head
She wagged her tail against the hearth.

Slowly as we left the room,
She turned her head to watch us go.
Hearing is the last sense to slow;
Her tail wagged faster as we spoke:
'Goodnight Waggie Maggie.'

Joan Woolley

It's A Dog's Life

My cushion sits in the kitchen
Just somewhere to lay my head.
To whom do you think I'm referring?
Yes - me! Molly the pooch and my bed.

This is where I spend my day
Because it's against the rule
To go where Tom and Matt must go
And that's to flaming school.

Dad and Mum have left for work
And now I'm all alone.
Nothing much to do all day
When I've ate my gravy bone.

Who's that ringing on the bell?
Woof, woof, woof! I howl
How dare they come and wake me up?
All I can do is scowl.

Ah! At last, I think I hear the boys
'Cause someone outside is making noise.
Perhaps Tom will give me some attention
Or Matt - some blooming aggravation!

Still, very soon I'll get my tea
And if it's nice, a walk maybe?
And later on, while watching telly
Mum might come and scratch my belly.

Then when it's getting very late
And everybody's yawning
They'll all tuck up in cosy beds
But I'm shoved in a crate till morning.
'Ugh!'

Lucy Mary Dean

Merlin

Merlin is our dearest friend
What a gift, what a Godsend
He came to us, so very small
Just a fluffy, furry ball.
Cute, pink nose and sparkling eyes
Full of wonder and surprise.

Now the fluffy ball has grown
Into our hearts and our home
Bringing with him great delight
Be it day, or be it night
Always eager for a snack
To disappear then come on back.

In the garden, in the house
Sleeping, playing with a mouse
Often begging to be let out
Especially when no one's about
What's that noise? What's that din?
Why it's Merlin wanting to come in!

At last, it is time to rest
It's the time I like the best
Even cats find time to sleep
Isn't it heavenly? - not a peep!

Gary Murphy

The Pleasure of My Company

Now listen guys,
I'll come and live with you on my terms.
This Stray Dogs' Home is OK, but I'm ready to up-size
To a pad more suited to my needs.
Here are my rules . . .
Number one, I don't chase balls, you can fetch instead,
Number two, I get to choose which side of the bed.
Next, I may bark at strangers if I can be bothered,
I shall expect thanks and praise, in kisses to be smothered.
On Sundays, when you cut the beef, I will be first in line,
Yorkshire pudding, meat and veg, will be absolutely fine.
I don't wake till I'm ready, though sometimes I just might
Want to go out in the garden in the middle of the night.
I suppose you can take me for rides out in the car,
But I will have the front seat and we mustn't go too far.
If the new armchair looks comfy, I insist you let me on,
Put newspaper there if you want to, but it won't be there for long.
Just bear in mind that I'm in charge - you do as I command.
I see by your face that you agree,
So lead me to that promised land!

Lindsey Priest

Kittens

Sitting by the window; on top of the tall, wooden fence,
Kittens, pretty and cute, one with black and white smudges,
Another all black with white mouth and whiskers.
Atop the fence, they look so surprised.
Quick, grab the camera, take a snap,
We'll make our own chances.
We push the curtain aside to flash the little kittens.
The seem to expect us
Looking and peer towards the window every time.
We do not view them long,
They are so active and endearing.
When daughter, on a visit, suggest the neighbours
May see our picture-taking efforts.
We are a lower level bungalow,
While house's upper windows oversee.
We've thought about it, true
And only hope their owner does not take them away.
We're enthralled when they appear,
So cheeky, so perky.
We are two oldies,
We hope we do not appear too quirky!

Betty Bukall

A Fine Specimen

A fine specimen of cat
Turned up at ours one day
Bright eyes, immaculate coat
Long legs like a greyhound, note
He asked if he could stay.

We enquired around the place
We then enquired wide
Did anyone lose a nice grey moggy
He's in good shape? We were told sorry
None are missing in the countryside.

We'd better feed the poor chap
We christened him, Toby
He always had a mysterious air
And fixed us with a familiar stare
We said let it so be.

Happily all lived together
And much time passed by
One day, leaning with the neighbour
Resting on the gate from labour
He put up the cry
'There's my feline buddy, Bert
You know, he appeared a while ago
Out of nowhere did he show
I feed him,' but we said, 'Whoa!
That's our cat!' 'Oh!'

Now Toby coolly eyes us up
Two homes he's made, for sure
It must be said that he's no fool
In fact, we feel he's quite a tool
Long may the boy endure.

Valerie Jenkins

To Mimi

Little cat,
As round on the cushion
As a cheese;
White face
Dainty as doily;
Movement
Sensuous as a tango,

You hold me captive
In one white paw.
Taking the deep chair
As your right
You abandon your
Beauty in its folds.

In thraldom I crave
Your purr or your
Caress. Tawny cat,
Astonishingly, once
You were lost,
But now I
Who adore you
Am lost.

Elsie Hamilton

The one We Call Smithie

When you were a baby
You fit into my hand
I bought you a stripy sweater
It was the best in all England.

Your best friend is Mr Monkey
He sleeps with you at night
You comfort chew his nose
With a nibble and a bite.

You have grown out of your sweater
And your bravery grows each day
You bark and howl to protect me
Squeaking your toy when you want to play.

Your nickname is Monkey Nose
You got that because you are cheeky
But your real name is the one you know
You are the one we call, Smithie.

Anne Prentice

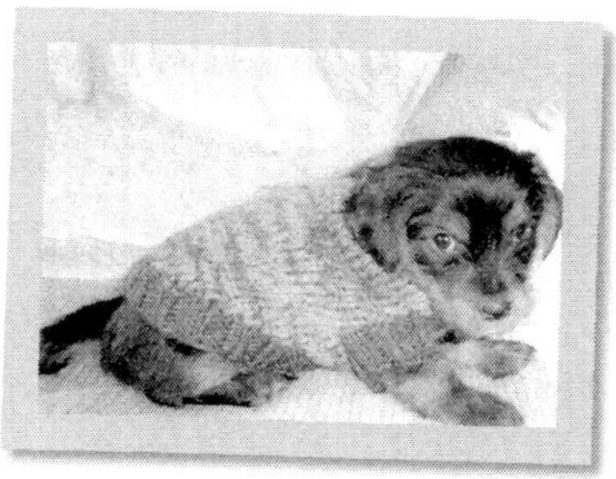

The Post office cat

'My cat was run over and killed last week.'
'How sad,' you said, 'it happens all the time,
But he was just a cat.'
No, he was not 'just a cat'.
He was Smudge, the Post Office cat,
Beloved by all.
Every morning he waited by the door
And when it opened, would march sedately in,
Tail erect and whiskers a-twitch.
Then with a quick bound, he would leap
Onto the wide window ledge,
Lord of all he surveyed.
He expected, and received,
The adoring pats and strokes
From all the customers.
When he felt that all was well with *his* Post Office,
He would stretch, arch his back
And jump silently to the floor,
Ready to cross the main road and wander home.
But not anymore, for now his nine lives have gone.
Rest in peace under the cherry tree,
Dear, dear Smudge.

Eve Turner

Cat

I cuddle this gorgeous creature in my arms
Tickle his furry tummy
What does he think of me?
Are those golden eyes full of love, or
Just anxious to be fed?
Does he know he can trust me?

It's his time for washing -
Don't interfere.
Utter concentration fills his mind.
Full of tricks, his agile beauty
Plays
To a rapt audience of one.

We have an understanding, cat and I -
I love him to distraction and
He lives with me.

Lilian Perriman

A Gift Given

Tegan, so bright
Her charm
Captivates and delights
Her bouncy ways
Her faithfulness
She conveys
A little dog
But love she brings
Wants are few
Colour, creamy and light
Her alertness sharp
A gift full of love
A treasure to share
To love her and to care
Helping me to find myself again
A gift given.

Maureen Thornton

Ben!

I went to jail for two long years
For a crime of wanton greed.
Sick with fear, I paid with tears
For that heinous, reckless deed.

No messages to ease the pain
And guilt I felt in me;
No letters came, I bore the shame
In default of sympathy.

My relatives, once filled with pride,
In me, their kith and kin;
Now blood denied, I'm classified
As an outcast for my sin.

The folk I saw as friends before
Now proved that they were not -
Concerned much more that I should go
And let myself get caught.

But even prison terms must end
And I was free at last;
To make amend and try to mend
The disasters of the past.

But still I felt a deep despair
Of paralysing grief,
Who was there would want to care
For a jailbird and a thief?

But I was wrong, for my disgrace
Meant nothing to my Ben -
He barked apace and licked my face
As he welcomed back his friend.

J Castel-Nuovo

Girlie

She never ever judged me
She never told me lies.
Was always there to welcome me
Love shining in her eyes.
Her nature was so sweet and true
A greater love I never knew.
When on human love I could never depend
She was there, at my side, until the end.
Licking away my tears
And with me through all the years.
Until her life on Earth was at an end
She always remained, my most trusted friend.
When the sad day came to part
Her love for me, stayed in my heart.
Her spirit with me, forever will stay
To help and guide me on my way.
Until the day I leave this plane
She and I will be together again.
United in love, forever and a day
Sweet Girlie and I will fly away.

Maureen Roberts

Misty

There she is, dozing in sun
Warm, content, too fat to run,
Birds no longer need to fear
You will pounce, so they come near,
Even mice are safe, far too fast
You cannot give chase as in past.

Your whiskers twitch, as you sleep
Dreaming little secrets you still keep,
Kitten days are now far away
Lithe and limber once was your play,
Stalking some imagined prey
Oh yes, but that was yesterday.

And now, you are content to lie
On warm sun-touched grass nearby,
Lazing in silent peace, with earth sun
In your favourite place, you sleep on.

T Webster

A Night out

Hustling hedgehog
Sniffles and whips
His nose past his toes
Over slimy trail trips.

Spines spiking up
Soft at their base
Delicate pink underbelly
Armour encased.

Eye, dark and short
Glinting jet glass
Whiffling wet nostrils
From side to side pass.

The tug of a worm
Stretched segments of juice
The crunch of a beetle
Shell crushed in a deuce.

The lick of an ant
The sugary spurt
Delicious young spider
Life-teeming dirt.

A night of delights
A grunt of success
Sweet composting bed
A mulch-hollowed rest.

Susan Thomas

Patch's Bath

Patch lay on the garden path,
He knew he needed a warm soapy bath.
Especially since he's rolled among
That stuff in the field with the terrible pong!

He'd sneaked in the kitchen and been thrown out,
By Mum, who was cooking some fresh rainbow trout.
And the presence of Patch had caused her to think,
The fish must be 'off' on account of the stink.

As he wondered how to escape this event,
There came up the path, a familiar old gent.
Grandad had come with his doggy pal, Mo,
For a fish and chip supper - he couldn't say, 'No!'

Patch wagged his tail, but all was not well,
For Mo turned away, when she picked up the smell.
His hatred of water and soft-scented soap,
Had spoiled all his plans for the pair to elope.

His dinner was placed outside the back door,
When she picked up his dish, Patch gave Mum a paw.
She took it and said that she'd fill up the tub,
So Patch went off meekly for a good, soapy rub.

When it was done and Patch was much drier,
He lay with his Mo, in front of the fire.
Being back with the family, rated higher than ten
And Patch vowed he'd never get smelly again!

Margaret Sanderson

Dear Mum

Each morning I get a cuddle
Then breakfast before your own,
You make my bed and clean the house
I've such a happy home.

After lunch, it's time for a nap
Then, if it's a sunny day
We go out into the garden
And have a lovely play.

I like the evenings best of all
Time to rest and watch, as you
Settle down with a book to read
Or watch TV with you.

Then, once again, it's time for bed
A cuddle, a kiss, that's that
I am affectionately yours
Thanks, from your tabby cat.
Love Topsy.

Barbara Dunning

My Pet

I have a little rabbit
Its name is Bobby Joe
I thought *he* was a buck
But *she* is a doe.
She has floppy ears
And runs around the floor
If I leave it open
She goes out the door.
Children like to stroke her
Because she's soft and warm
I always like to keep her
Safe from harm.
She's such a lovely pet
I love her very much
I let her sleep on my bed
Instead of inside her hutch.

E Riggott

Fluffy!

Fluffy, my rabbit,
Is seven years old,
She's grey and she's soft,
She's bright and she's bold.

She has glowing eyes
And a little twitchy nose,
The dearest bobtail
And soft fur, not clothes.

She likes to cuddle close to me,
She likes to be with her sister, Snowy,
She likes to eat and drink and sleep,
She likes to leap and stamp her feet.

She is big and very round,
She likes to curl up on the ground,
She likes to have a nice, soft bed,
Where she can lay her sleepy head.

She's the best, so let her be,
Because she is special to me
And I have to say,
I wouldn't have her any other way!

Gemma Musgrove

Bailey The Rabbit

Jan has a rabbit, keeps him in a hutch,
He really is a cutie, loved so very much,
But one morning, while rushing for his food,
The hutch door flew open and Bailey just fell out,
Jan wondered what the noise was,

As she came running out,
She stood there laughing
And laughed until she cried,
Bailey was lying, dazed, upon the ground,
Then she screamed, 'Jason!'
Bailey could have died,

Jan crept over and whispered in Bailey's ear,
Rabbit stew for tea,
Bailey jumped up from the ground
And started running round,
As if to say, 'There's nothing wrong with me!'

Pamela Page

Cat on My Lap

I am holding music in my hands,
fingertips touching the tremor,
treasure of melody unmade,
measure in warm fur
rolling from the belly of time
down through bone, into bone,
resonant, rich and round,
but with darker notes,
like perfume,
stealing into the marrow heart of me.

At my slightest touch
your deep contentment,
imminent,
lets loose, on tides of ebb and flow,
a low, murmuring lullaby
from another place,
an always place,
of affinity and knowing.

The more I stroke, the more your snuffle song
rattles and roars your frame,
as though your rocking tide will engulf us.
And then you sleep again,
stretching one slow, elegant paw,
with utmost deliberation and languor;
an invitation to paradise.
How can I refuse?

Shirley Wright

More Than A Pet

When I was ten, in the garden one day,
A kitten appeared and all I could say,
Was, she's tabby, she's cute, I want her for me,
I wasn't expecting to get her, you see.
The neighbour came out and heard what I said,
You can have her you know, so long as she's fed.
I ran to my parents and made a big fuss,
'Have her!' they cried, but look after her, you must.
That very same day, she came to my house.
We named her Latifa and bought her a mouse.
At first, she was shy and stayed in her box,
Then out she did come, attacking our socks.
Now I'm fifteen and surprising to me
I've acquired a companion as clever as me.
She sits on my clothes and sniffs at my shoes
But no matter what she does, I'm always amused.
When I was ten in the garden that day,
I could not have imagined what I'm about to say,
'Latifa, you mean the world to me!'

Laylah Ashour Abulafia

Discerning Companion

I'm a loyal, trusting canine friend
And know I'm very special
To my master.
I'm so happy to obey him; and enjoy his pleasure too,
But just sometimes I don't listen when he tells me what to do.
And now I'll share a secret, just with you:
I'm almost sure he's sometimes like that too!

Oh, that lovely pile of messy, fallen leaves
There by there hedgerow!
'Heel!' he ordered.
I played deaf; could not resist a dive in there - just to inspect -
Though I hate what always follows, that rub down to disinfect.
And here's my secret, don't you ever tell,
At times, he feels like I do here as well!

I admit he's often right
And so I cannot blame him
For the short leash.
But I so resent restriction that I pay him little heed.
I try pulling him along and sometimes tangle up the lead.
Again I share my secret just with you:
I do believe he's sometimes like this too!

Even though he loves his faultless Master - God -
And serves Him truly,
He's so like me!
So I guess we both are thankful for forgiveness full and free
And for loving reinstatement, too, within the family;
It's love like this that makes one so secure
He shares this feeling with me too, I'm sure.

Elma Heath

Tigger, The Recidivist Kleptomaniac Cat

He definitely isn't hungry,
We feed him well, you see

He likes a bit of fun,
He should really weigh a ton.

No cat as curious,
Has made people so furious.

Nothing at all is safe,
When he decides to feed his face.

Roast beef, a leg of lamb,
Or a juicy slice of ham.

He goes from door to door,
Stealing more and more and *more!*

If your windows are not closed,
While you're hanging out the clothes,

He'll take the opportunity,
(Showing no immunity)

To whisk away your dinner,
He really is a sinner.

We've tried to cure his habit,
But if he sees it, he'll nab it.

We tried 'home detention',
It only hardened his intention,

To become better at his game,
He feels no shame.
They're leaving, all our neighbours,
Because of his behaviour.

We hope they don't decide to sue,
We really don't know what to do!

Gaelynne Pound

Fig

A black and white stray
Came into our lives to stay,
A sanctuary, from whence he came
Fig, was his given name,

From neighbour's porch and our tree
Many a time, had to be set free,
Pouches of food, he'd help himself
Chew the packages, off the shelf,

Two years has long gone past
Settled down now with us, at last,
He's never ever let out at night
That loveable, adorable, black and white.

Gladys Brunt

Spider-Sophia, The Goblin Cat

She is about 113 years old
Her blue eyes, a transparent aquamarine,
Stare at you with a slight grin on her lipless mouth
Spider-Sophia is white with an orangey point on her tail
One of her ears, jiggery with scars
In her prime, she fought many toms who came to court her
She can fight
Once, she needed thirteen stitches;
One tough tom ripped open her chest
She will tell you of her glorious days, if you let her
Spider-Sophia is now mellowed and sleeps most of the day
She is a lady now
With her companion as her servant, she glides around the house
When she has displeased with her dinner, she summons her servant
'Goomer, what is this Meemeerrr!'
But Spider-Sophia is very content
She stares at you with icy-blue eyes and looks into your soul.

Yoko Hand

When Rabbits Go To Rainbow Bridge

(In loving memory of Lulu (3), died 3rd August 2006)

When rabbits go to Rainbow Bridge
Like dogs and cats and such,
These gentle creatures find their peace
For they are loved so much.

A place that's safe from traps and snares
And guns that maim and kill,
Where wounds are healed and fear is gone
And times are calm and still.

Where grass is long and lush and green
The rabbits hop about,
With twitching noses, bobbing tails
And ears that listen out.

Those rabbits who were treasured pets
Have loving folks on Earth,
Who cared for them and cuddled them
And knew a dear pet's worth.

Do rabbits go to Rainbow Bridge?
You bet your life they do!
Such sweet companions, cherished friends,
Deserve their Heaven too.

Brenda Maple

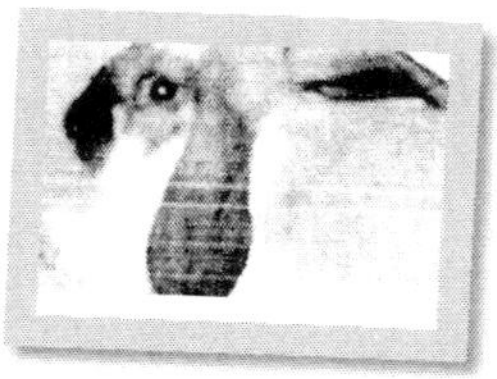

Not 'Just A Ferret'!

People may say he was just a ferret,
But he was a really good friend of mine
And I had this pet - just a ferret,
To love for too short a time.

He was a character called Trevor,
Just a ferret, as people could say,
But I played with him and nurtured him
And I wish I had him for one more day.

He was just a ferret, as people may say,
But we loved and lived together
And although I knew it couldn't last,
I wished he'd be with me forever.

I enjoyed each day I spent with this pet,
We were mates, right from the start,
Our years together, I'll never forget,
This little ferret just touched my heart.

My life will never be the same,
Because I can't ever see Trevor again.

Denise Jones

Goldfish

He swims around in his bowl,
My little soul of happiness,
Happy in his golden dress,
I feed him mealworms all compressed,
It must be quite lonely in there,
I hope he's not at all depressed,
I feed him daily,
So as not to get him stressed,
He seems to like it
And takes a bit
And waves his fins gaily,
Was he descended from
The Royal House of China Pond
With mighty Mandarin as guardian
With other goldfish in the garden,
He seems to be quite content,
Is this what peace and quiet meant?
I love to watch him basking,
When my day has been especially tasking,
That's why I find my pet goldfish so relaxing.

Alan Pow

Trixie, The Buck Rabbit

The rabbit was white with flat ears on his head
We put the small bundle of fur in the shed
With the chickens and soon they became friends;
In the morning we found him roosting with the hens.
But we grew tired of the chicks and soon they were gone
And the poor little rabbit was all forlorn.
It was not long before he stopped being sad
Because he made friends with the dog and the cat.
He chased around with Puss and played ball with Pips
He was aptly named Trixie 'cause he was full of tricks.
He slept under the garage on a summer's night
But in the winter he showed he was really bright.
He'd sit by the door until Master came back
Then quickly slipped inside and settled on a sack.
Sometimes he went up the road, walking on his own
He had a look around and then returned home.
At eight years old he strolled outside once more
When a huge Great Dane appeared he had not seen before.
His mistress ran out and shooed off the dog
But by then poor Trixie was in deep shock.
He was put in Pip's basket, who tried in vain
To warm the rabbit and revive him again
This is the true story of Trixie, our pet
Whom we loved dearly and will never forget.

Lisa Wolfe

The Policeman And The Cat

I had to take my cat to the vet,
He was an obstreperous pet,
Though I tempted him with chicken,
With salmon and cream,
He plainly ignored me
And caused me to scream.

I thought, I know, I'll think like a fox,
So I found an old cardboard box,
My cat then went in,
I tied it with string,
Topped off with a ginormous knot.

We nearly got to the vet's surgery,
When blow me, if he didn't get free,
He hissed and he spat,
He wasn't my cat,
He thought me his arch enemy.

He was trying to do me great harm,
So I fended him off with an arm,
I near crashed the car,
As I stopped not so far,
From a PC watching us in alarm.

The policemen asked could he help
As I shouted to him, 'Save yourself,
My cat's gone berserk
And I'm late for work,
I fear for my cat's mental health.'

The policeman said, 'It's OK, I can assist,
Cats find me hard to resist.'
And as he opened the door,
My cat proffered a paw
And his mad behaviour did suddenly desist.

'That's amazing,' I said, 'Do you find,
That you're telepathically using your mind,
To calm and assure
With your knowledge of law?'
He joked, 'They just know I'm feline kind.'

Sheila Gee

A Case of Mistaken Identity

In case you haven't noticed,
I'm a rabbit, not a dog.
I really like to skip and hop,
Not to walk or jog.

Why on Earth do you insist,
On reaching for the lead?
Dragging me around the yard,
Is the last thing that I need.

So, if you want a pet that,
Fetches or plays dead,
Go back to the pet shop and
Buy one that can be led.

For I feel so ridiculous,
Because you make me wear,
That revolting harness,
It's a rabbit's worst nightmare!

Helen Moulton

An Elderly Cat

The house and garden I rule with glee,
Any imposter must get past me
A squirrel, a bird, a cat or a mouse,
They'll get no welcome near my house.

Too old for a fight, a hiss will suffice
The fun of a chase I've had to sacrifice

Catching the birds I no longer do,
I'm much too old for that hullabaloo.

It's easy these days to get my own way,
Preferring to snooze for most of the day.

Food on demand with love thrown in,
There's never a need to scavenge in the bin.

As I lie in the flower bed, sun on my fur,
I charm them all with a snore and a purr.

At fifteen years old, with love to give,
It's an easy life for as long as I live.

Margaret Perry

A Faithful Friend

The watchful shepherd crossing the moor,
His crook assisting his long-paced strides
Alert of ear and keen of eye
His faithful black and white collie by his side.

The sheepdog watching every move
Listening eagerly for his master's command
Bringing the large flock safely home
Down to the low, more sheltered land.

Gentle, good-tempered, loyal and willing
Through biting winds and driving snow
Nell has rescued many a life
The slightest movement and she will know.

Waiting for new lambs to be born
It seems the vigil will never end
Their lifelong partnership has found a bond
Twixt man and his ever faithful friend.

Greta Craigie

Experiment on A Cat

Every morning I expect the black
and white cat to fall in the filling bath.
she flirts with fate, balancing
on the slippery edge and reaching down
to take a lick of steaming water.
her broad bum faces me
and it would be the easiest thing
to give her a little shove,
just enough so she'd lose balance and slide in.
I'm interested to know what she'd do,
after the initial shock.
Would she rise from the deep like the shark in *Jaws?*
Or would she perhaps discover that fear
of water is an inherited whim? She might
suddenly realise that weightlessness
is rather pleasant and pussy-paddle around,
her thick coat plastered to her spine,
the black swim-cap of her head,
the seal's whiskers, her sea-green eyes
gazing up at me as if to say,
come on in, it's lovely.

Ann Kelley

For Leo

Over the rainbow
Through angel's clouds
A beautiful soul
Is Heaven-bound
And his eternal peace is found
A beautiful soul
Touched my heart with such love
And is forever returned
To his soul up above
A beautiful soul
Who can now run and play
With such love all around
In eternity he will stay
And when fate plays its part
And unites our hearts
Together again we will be
Our spirits at peace and free
To that beautiful place I will go
And spend eternal bliss
With my Leo.

Dawn Serbert

My Faithful Friend

My little Border terrier whose coat is black and tan
Above his nose has spikes of fur - guess his name if you can!
That's right - we call him Spike - indeed he knows his name quite well
He knows the sound of every knock or ring on our doorbell.
He welcomes all with a wagging tail and leaps up in delight
When visitors come to the house in daytime or at night.
He loves to walk down country lanes whilst straining on his lead,
He loves his toys and food as well and scoffs his lunch with greed.
He hates the vacuum and the mop, but stands still in his bath,
He growls at all the larger dogs who try to cross the path.
Stretched out before the open fire with one eye on TV
When horses, dogs or cats come on, he lets out *woofs* of glee,
He wonders why they have no smell, as he sits close to the screen,
But when I walk into the room, his lovely eyes will gleam.
They shine with faithfulness and love, a pleasure to behold
Spike's really full of mischief but can be as good as gold.
He loves to chew my cushions when he thinks my back is turned
He doesn't like me going out - he's glad when I've returned.
If I say, 'Come!' or maybe, 'No!' the look upon his face
Says, 'No, I won't,' or 'Perhaps I might,' as he runs around the place.
But when he stands in front of me, his paws upon my knee
I'm sure there are no better friends, than Spike, my dog and me.

Enid Hewitt

Missy, My Cat

She's like a little soldier
So loyal to me
Following me around from room to room
And when I sweep the floor
She plays with the broom
She thinks the mop is a spider
And tries to bite it
But she's no fool
She's a very intelligent cat
And leaves me in no doubt of that
And she's a bit of a menace
When I sit down to watch the telly
As she starts to scratch
And thinks of her belly
She gives me a paw, when I get the ham out
So we have to spell it out
But I swear - she's learnt how to spell
As she follows me to the fridge
And she's such a beautiful
Feisty, furry tabby cat
And not at all fat.

Chriss Angel

A Shared Friend - 'Spencer'

Spencer was my son's dog,
He often came to stay,
We loved each other dearly,
He knew which games to play.

He would sit quietly in my kitchen,
Waiting for a morsel to drop,
Then he would nick my tea towel
And chase up the stairs to the top.

When I called and apprehended him,
He would disappear under the bed,
And stopped there, motionless,
Pretending to be dead.

Eventually he sneaked back to his basket,
Leaving the tea towel behind,
To join all the other spoils he had encountered,
Shoes, socks, tights, he managed to hide.

He loved all the home comforts,
Our sofa with throw he liked best,
And sometimes he disappeared up the stairway,
To take an afternoon rest.

He caused havoc and confusion,
When poaching my grandson's favourite toy
One day he retrieved newly planted roses,
Not exactly a very good ploy.

Then, one day I wakened calling his name,
In my dreams he had vanished in a tunnel of mist,
Soon after, my son telephoned to tell me,
Poor Spencer had died suddenly, without a parting kiss.

Ann-Rose Harris

Arthur

Your constant demands drive me crazy
You're overfed and downright lazy
You hog the bed and the best chair
You stroll through life without a care
You're top cat and it's plain to see
You certainly found a mug in me.

Rachel McKie

Rude Awakening

There's a cockerel hereabouts who doesn't know the time,
He's not aware that waking us, is truly such a crime.
However, this is countryside and it's a natural noise,
Not like roaring aeroplanes or other screaming toys.
He's welcoming the dawn of day, greeting all his hens,
Not killing people with bloody weapons, or grey, metallic Brens.
His punishment may end the same, with death as his reward,
Just as if he'd murdered with dagger or with sword.
It seems so very cruel, you know, to feast upon the cock,
When all he's done that could be wrong, is just misread the clock.

Christine Bridson-Jones

Fat cat

Don't say the F word in front of Paws,
She'll take offence and show her claws.
She thinks that she's a slinky cat,
Without a trace of feline fat.
She doesn't know with every stride,
Her belly swings from side to side
And if she knows, she won't admit
It wobbles when she tries to sit.

The vet said she's a beautiful cat,
A shiny coat and all of that,
But reprimanded me and hubby
For having a cat that's, 'A wee bit chubby!'
She said we'd have to watch her weight
And make a note of all she ate.
She really needs to be on a diet,
We said we'd go ahead and try it.

We tried our best to be quite strict,
But the sneaky cat, she'd got it licked.
It took a while, but then we learned,
As soon as both our backs were turned,
She'd creep up to her sister's dish
And grab a mouthful of her fish.
Then slink away to somewhere quiet
To make a mockery of the diet.

Needless to say, after weeks of trying,
The stubborn cat is still defying,
Our every effort to make her see
That 'round' isn't how she's meant to be!

Jane Hill

Lucky-Duke

We had snow the first week after I brought you home
Fifteen years ago, you didn't turn tail and run back indoors
Bless your little hide, no!
You were a mere twelve inches up to your ears,
The snow was eight inches deep,
But you kept plodding on without any fears
You wanted to take a peep
To see what this strangeness was in your backyard,
It smelled cold and it was and the water was hard
Where it had dripped from the gutter and froze,
So I said, 'Come on, let's take you in,
Or you'll get a chill in your toes!'
You'd sleep through the night, up to six or seven hours,
You were clean from five months of age,
I'd put newspaper down, but you'd need less and less,
Till you didn't even need half a page,
The problem was water, but not 'puppy pee'
As you tried to catch hold of your reflection,
You thought, *who's this in my water bowl?*
This needs some further inspection!
You changed all your teeth (I've still got a few),
You never had any trouble, you had your own mitten
To pull on or chew,
Yes, I've some kept in a little plastic 'bubble',
Now you're fifteen and laid snoring,
Of what do you dream?
Your cat pal called 'Spike' who's now seven,
Or when you've a saucer each from a carton of cream
And your face seems to say,
'Bow-wow! This is Heaven!'

Christine May Turner

Trilby And The Angel You Became

The day you came into my life
A scraggly, leggy thing
Little did I know back then
Just how much joy you'd bring

As you grew, your beauty grew too
As you ran so wild and free
And I'll never forget, my darling girl
The loving way you'd nuzzle me

The first time I sat upon your back
And gently stroked your mane
You seemed to know just what to do
To take away my pain

We grew together
The perfect partnership people would say
To always have you in my life
I used to hope and pray

I never really thought you'd leave
You seemed to love me so much
The way you'd look, the way you'd whinny
At my every touch

But it wasn't to be
You were too beautiful for this life
My darling little angel
You left me in such strife

That day I came to see you
And you were lying on your side
I knew almost straight away
I would never again ride

The vet, so kind
Took me aside and said it was cruel
To keep you alive in so much pain
To do that, I would have been a fool
My arms around you
Tears again soaking your neck
I knew I had to say goodbye
But I was such a wreck

And even now, as I write this
Tears filling my eyes
I find it hard to think of good times
But we definitely had our highs

The first competition we won
You, my angel, so good
Behaved so perfectly
Just like I knew you would

I miss you, Trilby
More and more each day
It's eight years since I last held you
And the pain still won't go away

I will never forget you, my baby
And in my heart you'll always be
The only comfort I have now
Is that from your pain, you're free.

Liz Argent

My Mum

Having children would have been fun
And I would have been a good mum
But our mum is getting old and only has Jet and me,
So I had an operation
So that I could not have any babies
Although it made Mum very sad,
But it was for the best and now I am older myself,
I do not mind, because our home is full of love.

Jet agrees with me, that we have the best home,
Because there is a comfy bed
And there is plenty of food and treats,
So we are lucky living with our old mum,
Who sometimes is very slow,
So we just take it in turns to look after her,
Jet likes to wait for us at the end of the lane
When we come home from a walk,
He would like to come as well,
But Mum said no, because it is dangerous for puss
But we all walk home down the lane together
Because we are a family, with lots of love.

Julia Leonie Holden

Wallis - Best Friend

Planting flowers with Wallis
Is such a lot of fun
She's digging right behind me
And what I've done's undone!

Barking at the postman
When the mail comes through the door,
Picking up the letters
As they fall upon the floor.

Lying in her basket,
Lazing in the sun,
One eye open, one eye shut
Just to see who's come.

Playing in the meadow
Crouching in the grass,
She thinks she's in the World Cup
With a right, deft-footed pass.

Knowingly she watches
Jumping in my chair
Taking full possession
When she knows that I'm not there.

Joyful is her greeting
When I come home and see
Her waiting by the doorstep
She's always there for me.

Belinda Eddy

Barney Boy

(My pride and joy)

Barney, my terrier
Follows me everywhere
He struts around me
Without a care.

Chasing the moggies
He's a passionate doggy.
He chews my possessions
Leaves them torn and soggy.

An affectionate soul
With a coat of red-gold,
He whimpers and whines
When he's tied to the pole.

He barks at the children
In order to warn them -
That they could be bitten
If they mess with him!

He's a little treasure
Who brings me great pleasure.
When I feel down
This dog reassures.

Ever ready for a fight
He has never taken flight.
Protective of his territory
He guards the house both day and night.

Wolfing down his mixer and meat
Begging for his favourite treats
My companion and best friend
Without him, my life's incomplete.

George Lionrock

Meerkats

Meerkats,
Queer cats,
Are you really there, cats?
On your haunches
Guarding your den
Gone in a flash
In your hole
Then

Whiskers peep out
You all club together,
One is on watch
Guarding the kittens
Whether
There are foes about.

The rest search for snacks to munch -
Scorpions, beetles, snakes
Hold them in tiny hands to crunch.

Meerkats
Like Siamese
Are you proper cats
Or
Just
A wheeze?

Jane Mccarty

Black Mischief

Fair specimen of the feline clan,
You'd gladden the heart of any man.
My eye must wonder at your sleekness,
But my skin has doubts about your meekness!
While other cats I'd pet and tickle,
I'm wary with a dame so fickle!
You'll take some petting, if inclined,
But woe betide if you change your mind.
Caressing hands, caught unaware,
Are doomed when claws you quickly bare.

With royal gait you pace the floor,
Disdain oozing from every pore.
Not for you to rub again' us,
In appreciation of good dinners -
You barely condescend to nibble.
Such airs are quite incorrigible!

And how you dote on all that grooming -
See the brush and you go zooming
Up the hallway, down the stairs:
'You'll not drag that thing through my hairs!'
But when it's time for your daily daunder,
Down the hallway you will wander,
Sit upon your dignity
Until someone should chance to see.
And when the leash is round your neck,
You surely don't move fast, by heck;
Out the door, a streak of light,
In half a tick, we're out of sight.
Hauteur cast off, just like that -
No more a queen, you're just a cat!

Hilary Aziz

our Special Dog

Our special dog's name is Precious
She is very playful and funny too
The kids really enjoy her antics
Let me tell you about a few

My daughter, Chaunte, sat on the sofa
Eating a sandwich this particular day
When Precious jumped on the end table
Ran on the sofa and took Chaunte's sandwich away

My son, Marcus, is somewhat disabled
And Precious takes advantage of him I dread
He left a sandwich on the computer table
Precious ate the meat, but left him the bread

When at the dinner table, Precious had no favourites
She go under the table, hoping for food to fall
She went from child to child for handouts
She'd get so full, she couldn't come when you called

Poor Marcus would take Precious outside for exercise
But when he wanted her to come back in
She'd look at him and just continue to run around
If he tried to catch her, she knew she would win.

William Lacewell, Jr

My Pup

Puppies are lovely to cuddle
With coats all soft and smooth
You forgive them for making a puddle
They sit down and don't want to move

Those lovely eyes can say so much
She is the sweetest pup for me
Sniffing at the rabbit in the hutch
Wagging her tail for all to see

Off to the moors when she gets older
I am sure she will enjoy all the fun
Every day she is getting bolder
When I take her out for a run.

Phyllis Nichols

Man's Best Friend

(Dedicated to FAITH - For Animals In Trouble there's Hope)

When God had made the Earth and sky
The flowers and the trees
He then made the animals
And all the birds and bees

When all his work was finished
Not one was quite the same
He said, 'I'll walk this Earth of mine
To give each one a name.'

He then travelled land and sea
And everywhere he went
A little creature followed him
Until his strength was spent

When all were named upon the Earth
And in the sky and sea
The little creature said, 'Dear Lord
There's not one left for me.'

The Father smiled and softly said,
'I left you to the end
I've turned My own name back to front
So you're called 'Dog', my friend.'

Frank Harper

Toffee

Still I can see her dear
Patient, old face, tortoiseshell
In colour and her warm topaz eyes.
Rescued from a rubbish tip
Where a whole litter she had raised,
She showed eternally her gratitude
And her affection, just for me.
I brought her mother-heart, a tiny kitten -
Black and white, with bounding energy.
After the first short panic of surprise
Toffee adopted Micky too;
Licked him and cuffed him,
Loved him as her own.
When she died, he felt bereft
And my heart throbbed with grief.
I gaze upon her picture now
And remember her with love
Mixed with an ache of unshed tears.

Mary Pledge

Gem

(Dedicated to a dear little dog who is truly a gem)

It was three long years since my dog had died
And I vowed I'd have no other
And then a dog rescue rang me up
And I began to discover
So many dogs were needing homes
So many dogs were lost
And they told me of you - so desperate
So then I counted the cost
You were thirteen years old and totally deaf
And your eyes were failing too
With cataracts in both of them
So nobody wanted you
Yes - you were old and deaf and going blind
And that's the reason why
Your folk put you on a rubbish tip
And left you there to die
And so it was you came to me
And I will always endeavour
To love you, as you should be loved
And I will leave you never
No more will you be lost and cold
And never more you'll roam
I'll love you forever and a day
My little 'Gem' you're home.

I G Beattie

The White Horse

Standing feet upon the gate
I lean to look inside, quite late
To espy the gentle silky horse
Nibbling softly midst the gorse
With velvet, limpid, moon-like eyes
His coat so white
I throw an apple at him
By surprise
To see if he would wander in
Towards me for a tickle on the chin

The gentle pony, white as snow
Frivolous tail swishing to and fro
With shiny mane standing nonchalant there
Standing so tall, without a care

I love the white horse in the quiet field
I love the white horse standing on the Weald
I love the white horse with all of my might
I love the white horse, he is my delight.

Margaret Bennett

A Dog's Life

Curled snug and warm, gently snoring.
Then, *Yap! Yap! Yap!* snarl at postie,
Gnashers ripping his precious delivery.
I've seen off the enemy once again!

Now my daily slither across the itch-relieving mat.
The door opens and I have to go walkies.
I turn tail and retreat to cottage warmth,
Driven back by drips on my coat.
But we need to stroll and chat to neighbours.
I get fed up and start to sing,
This usually helps to speed the chat.
Back in the nest and rub of the towel,
Grabbed by my teeth for a tug-of-war.

I'll sneak in the kitchen
And steal Kitty's food.
Then, out in the garden
To sniff and dig treasure.
And no one will know
Save the smudge on my nose.

Up to the third step, where morning sun glints
I rest above warm pipes and am still for a while.

If I sit doe-eyed as they eat their lunch
I may steal a morsel from soft-hearted Dad
But a rock hard biscuit is my only reward
I hop up the stairs and bury it deep
In a wardrobe full of shoes and bags
After that, I leap on the bed and snooze under duvet
Till discovered by Mum
I am scolded again but know in my heart
They love me from my nose to my tail.

Wendy Brooks

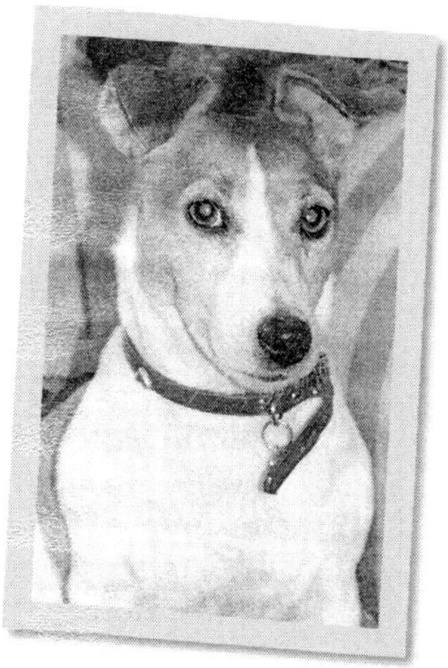

Gem

To most, she was only a dog
But to me, she was my best friend!
No more rambles in the woods will we take
Or games of hide-and-seek behind giant oaks will we play
No more walks on winter mornings
Over sodden fields will we roam
No more hills together shall we climb?

To most, she was only a dog
But to me, she was my best friend!
Her toys lay dormant beside her empty bed
Her lead still hangs on the hook in the cupboard
I haven't the heart to take it down
The foot of my bed where she used to lie
Is cold and bare.

To most, she was only a dog
But to me, she was my best friend!
She was my protector when I was afraid
My shadow when I was fine
My confidant when I was in need
My hot-water bottle when I was cold
To most she was only a dog
But oh God! To me she was my best friend!

Esme Eckett

Little Treasures

Dawn arrives too quickly on a mid-October day,
I feel no 'up and go' - the reason why, I cannot say.
Reluctantly, I look out on a blustery autumn morn,
In my bed I'd like to stay, so cosy and so warm!

My refreshing morning shower fails to alter how I feel
And down the stairs I go, to prepare my morning meal.
Movement can be heard behind the kitchen door,
Two little faces greet me - my heart begins to soar.

I'm welcomed by two little dogs, their faces all aglow,
Their excitement at my presence never fails to show.
Such joy I feel at seeing them; I'm lost for words to say,
But I'm glad I made the effort to get up from bed today!

Anticipation peaks, as breakfast done, we're on our way
And once again life seems worthwhile, much brighter is my day.
No looking back or feeling glum, the country lane we walk,
My pets, I know, feel just the same - if only they could talk!

The simple things of life that give me so much pleasure;
The love from dear little pets is something 'rich' to treasure.
Some would give the very world to have such joy as this,
For, thanks to my companions, my life is sheer *bliss!*

Vivienne Vale

Fearless Kit

Four tiny paws,
with dagger-like claws
Fearless little thing,
That can fly without wings.
Leaping over walls without a pause for thought,
If danger lies ahead,
Pray, you won't end up dead.
Only the bird in your mouth,
On which your anger you take out.
Fearless little thing,
But what great joy you bring.
When you demand attention,
I give you affection
And when you purr on my lap,
I'm really *your* pussycat.

Malisa Perriton

My Family Pet

I express my love for a cat,
Which was my family pet,
She was always contented,
Until she was to see the vet.

My family pet was called Sootie,
She grew to be so fat
And all she did was to amuse herself,
Falling asleep on the mat.

Sadly, she's no longer with us,
Cos she passed away
And I really miss her being around,
More and more each day.

Louise Chafer

Lord Cassidy

My name is Cassidy
Born with four legs, now have three
Abandoned, left to roam
Nowhere I could call my home

Scavenged to keep alive
Till the day I nearly died
Fast car hit my back leg
In the gutter, left for dead

A kind soul passed my way
Called the RSPCA
One of my nine lives lost
Amputation was the cost

It did not take me long
To recover good and strong
Two ladies came to see
If they liked the look of me

Skinny, with stitches in
Both their hearts I strove to win
How I turned on the charm
Cradled in one lady's arm

Here lives Lord Cassidy
In the lap of luxury
Warm, well-fed, safe and sound
Pampered and extremely round

Physically disabled
My story will be fabled
Great trauma opened doors
I've landed on my three paws!

Pauline Ilsley

My Big, old Ginger Cat, Tom

I was sitting, waiting to see the vet
When in came a lady with her aunt's old pet
His owner had died, but no one wanted him to keep
In this cardboard box, brought in to be put to sleep.

I said, 'I'll have him, if the vet checks him over and says he is well'
How old he was, no one could tell
He came home with me, but was muddled and scared
He wanted his Mistress, for whom he'd cared.

He hid under my sofa, but I did get him fed
Spent the next four weeks on my spare bed
I got him a collar and took him outside
He sniffed round, jumped on the fence and decided to hide.

I had trained him to come to be fed, by ringing a bell
He'd caught on quite quick and was doing well
While I anxiously waited for him to come home
He remained lost to me, out on the roam.

We had postered the area, he'd been locked in a shed
When he found himself free, he dashed back to be fed
He'd finally realised where he was to live
He was so happy and loving, loud purrs he would give.

He was Ginger, long in the body and such a long tail
For a drink in the sink, he'd let out such a wail
Until his last days, he loved his final home
I miss that old softy, now that he's passed and gone.

Sheila Bates

Bessie

She came into my life like a ball of fur
A bundle of fluff without a care
She seemed to say, 'I am what you see
And that's the way it's going to be.'
She won me over from that very first day
When she let me know she would have her own way
She cheers me up if I get low
It is as though she seems to know
She is my best friend, so loyal and true
Bessie Beach, I will always love you.

Robert Beach

Animals

I'm only a harmless creature
I've got feelings just like you
So why do they keep me locked up
In a place they call *the zoo?*

I'd love to have my freedom
To roam over the country wide
But they've locked up all the gateways
To keep me and my pals inside

One day, the gates may be opened
And we will be free to roam
But we may still be strangers
For we may be far from home.

Pat Adams

My cat

Rain again!
Skies as grey as my cat's grey fur,
Clouds as grim as his accusing face -
My fault, of course - I know he thinks it,
Blames me for weather I can't prevent.
Crouched by the door, he watches the downpour,
Then runs to the front to find the same.
His narrowed eyes look into my eyes
Their burning amber almost veiled,
Then widen as sudden noise attracts him;
He jumps on the sill to find the source -
He snickers his menace at something he sees,
Something hidden to my searching eyes -
But hackles rising and whiskers twitching
He continues to yowl his feline challenge.
A full five minutes his attention is riveted,
Till gradually weariness overcomes him
And, paws tucked under, he settles to rest.
Purring comfortably, he drifts off to slumber
And peace descends with his sleeping breath.

Ann Dodson

Cat

Tailor-made frost on winter trees,
Blued the nose, roughed the knees.
Small tiger kitten, gaunt of frame,
Huddled by the gate, shivered again.
Master of the house, finishing his day,
Found the kitten, where it lay.
Took it inside, where on a warm mat,
Another tiger, dear, sleek, old cat,
Elderly lady of twenty years,
Licked away the kitten's fears.
Now small kitten, how you've grown,
Repaying with love the kindness shown.
Two sleek tigers, there on the mat,
Four green eyes, cat by cat.
Out of the cold she came
And in our hearts she'll remain.

Ruth Allerston

Getting The Bird

Our cat is laying behind the conifer tree,
On her face is an expression of sheer ecstasy,
Suddenly she moves one ear, then keeps perfectly still,
On the garden path there is a bird and our cat is ready to kill,
Unaware of its plight, the little bird starts to sing,
The cat unfurls its lithe body and gets ready to spring,
But the little bird seems to sense that something is wrong
And stops singing her pretty little song,
The cat picks up on the little bird's fright,
She begins to purr loudly in her delight,
The end of her tail gives a little twitch
And her position she has to switch,
She nestles back further in the tree, now she is almost invisible
And now she can't be seen at all,
Suddenly, she pounces, sure of catching her prey,
I know it's only nature, but I have to turn away.

Then I hear the bird singing and everything is fine,
When I look, I see her perched, safely on my washing line.

All at once, the cat runs in, looking a bit unsure
And watches a heron eating our pond fish,
Safely from behind our patio door,
The little bird watches as well, then gives a little chirp
And flies away quite happily, leaving our cat feeling like a twerp!

Maureen Arnold

'Chou-Chou', The Clever Poodle

Dear little Emily,
Now you are *six* -
Best friend of 'Chou Chou' -
Still up to his tricks!
Who's that a-knocking
On my front door?
Perhaps someone's joking! -
It's a quarter to four!
Good gracious! It's 'Chou-Chou'!
He's waiting right there -
Rush past me? Oh no!
He'd never ever dare!
He waits till it's 'Come in'
Then by me he trots,
Always obedient,
We all love him - lots.
He still likes to tease us,
Hiding balls in our shoes
Or else 'neath the sofa
Next to which he will snooze.
His girlfriend is 'Phoebe'
Frisky and bold.
They're happy together
And as good as gold,
Tails wagging constantly
As they romp and they play,
Cuddly and friendly -
With Poodles we'll *stay!*

Valma June Streatfield

Harry, The Cat

He's big, he's black and looks fearsome
With baleful yellow-green eyes
He can just barely squeeze through the cat flap
And he doesn't much care where he lies

You can find him curled up like a kitten
Or proudly he sits like the Sphinx
Sometimes stretched out like a lion
Or ready to pounce like a lynx

His favourite food is tinned tuna
He can pick up the scent in a flash
Don't offer him cheap lumpy cat food
You'd just be wasting your cash

He lets you know when he's hungry
Complains like a grumpy old man
Not keen on using the cat flap
Makes you open the door when he can

In summer he's found in the sunshine
When his fur takes a gingery hue
In winter he's right by the fire
No room there for me or for you

But he's ours and we all love him dearly
Even though he won't sit on your lap
He's got some white whiskers and is long in the tooth
But still is a handsome old chap.

Kim Castle

Cracker

That Cracker is a clever cat there can really be no doubt;
She'll always find a comfy spot whether inside or out.
She never likes to be too cold or hot
Always finds the ideal spot.

Morning sees her on the garden seat,
Tail tucked round all nice and neat;
When she hears us run the tap in the sink
She'll yawn and stretch and coyly blink,

Then saunter over picking her route,
To spring onto the window sill at the toot.
She rubs her face against the frame -
'Come on - let me in! Just play the game!'

As soon as the key clicks in the door,
She's through to her dish requesting more;
But always before beginning to feed,
Gives a nudge and a purr - 'Many thanks indeed!'

When Beth sits down to have her lunch,
Cracker somehow has this hunch
That lands her close to cheese and Marmite -
Which she eats from Beth's hand - a comical sight.

She'll take a stroll to beat her bounds,
Watch for movement, listen for sounds,
Of interesting, tiny, furry prey
To help her pass her leisurely day.

The sparrows and blackbirds chirp and scold,
They know her hunting tricks of old;
Even so some young birds still get caught,
Before, by parents, they've been well taught.

But Cracker goes her own sweet way,
Snoozes, strolls and feeds to pass the day.
Evening often means sliding onto Beth's lap,
For a stroke and a purr - and another wee nap.

Deryck Southgate

Twinkle

That dear little dog of mine,
I can't help writing about her,
One eye open, one eye closed,
Lying in front of the fire.

I know what will wake her up,
I'll say the magic word,
She's not made a move,
Perhaps she never heard.

I know what I'll do,
I'll rattle her lead loud,
That's done the trick,
Of her I'm very proud.

Off we go, down the road,
Folk say nice things about her,
Sniffing every blade of grass,
This walk could take an hour.

We have walked about a mile,
She'd like to walk some more,
I think that will be enough,
My feet are getting sore.

Got back home, must sit down,
I really do feel tired,
Must not say that word again,
For a couple of hours.

Two hours later she looks at me,
Twinkle, not again,
Give me another half an hour,
I'll be rested then.

Jeff Northeast

My Friend

He doesn't know I'm ugly, he doesn't know I'm fat,
That I have bad habits, or suffer this or that.
He's faithful and so loving, and always there for me,
He protects me from all strangers, guards me as all can see.
Happiness surrounds us both, warmth from him when near,
My friend so true and loyal is my dog, so loved, so dear.
I let him know I love him, I let him know I care,
My time, though very precious, I insist he has his share.
We communicate with each other, I understand his 'talk',
Companions forever, until the final walk.

Patricia Evans

Bert, The Budgie

Bert is my budgie
He's crazy, that's a fact,
He jumps off his perch
And lands right on his back

He rolls around from left to right
His legs up in the air,
He stays like that for quite a while
He really doesn't care

You give him some water,
He'll run up and down
There's a look on his face
I am sure I see a frown

Where's my food? he almost says
Chirping like he's mad,
Should you walk away from him?
No that will make him sad

Have some patience, wait a while,
I'm sure this bird, is a child!
Fed and watered, it's time for bed
Now he wants to play instead

Bert, oh Bert
You drive me mad
With all your noise and mess
But you're the one
In the whole wild world
I really love the best.

Sheila Johanson

Rescue

Little and scared he was, all fun of life
Gone with the fearless youth he briefly knew,
Bright eyes haunted by experience
Of those things which science without a heart can do.
Made for loving, his still-adoring eyes
Searched my own for a sign that he was safe.
Still in his canine soul, he dared to hope:
In my heart old wounds began to chafe.

Hadn't I built a prison of my own
And known the same hunted fear of life's strong hand?
But I had grown bitter, turned from my own kind,
Grown old, untrusting, unable to understand,
While this small creature - helpless as I was not -
Had somehow escaped because he knew he must,
And with his adoring eyes explained to me
All things are possible if we still trust.

Little and scared was I, all fun of life
Gone with the fearless youth I briefly knew.
A small dog's pleading opened my prison door,
A small dog's courage led my spirit through;
For in that esteem we feel for one another
We renew ourselves, our stricken world extends,
We revere all life, our sister and our brother.
Trust is the doorway where the prison ends.

Pamela Constantine

Till Spring, Until Then

A flurry of fur grey, comes every single day
the visitor begs outside the doors
exquisite little face, expressive cute paws.

Peanuts, custard creams, most buried whole
tulips, hyacinths upended, a favourite delight
the daffodils, too, follow a similar plight
this bold cheeky scrap knows where to scrounge
when from kitchen, seeking attention, a failure
fidgets, looks in appealing, patio by the lounge.

Beware, danger lurks on the carpeted floor
slit-eyed, jet-black, panther-like cat
obsessively jealous, paranoiac territorial
fangs mean, fast and all that
with matchless agility, run, squirrel run
trust him not, climb high the trees
for when hunting a useless command
come down at once... Oscar please . . .

Considered a pest the squirrel
born the wrong shade, so they say
to me enchanting, the loveable scamp every day
in the long silence of winter
when you tuck down in bed
bulbs to bloom the borders returned
and tools go back in the shed.

Silence is lonely, the garden without you, bare
Oscar sleeps by radiators, possibly in dreams
on safari, big game hunting there
Till spring, little one when full of fun you rise
a midwinter glimpse before welcome, well maybe
until then, I look forward, your image again in my eyes.

Mildred F Barney

Ginny - My Lovely Cat

I had a ginger cat once
She died at the age of seventeen
She was the cutest bundle of fur
You had ever seen
She had her moments
So, she's a cat -
They are independent
What's wrong with that?
She would curl round your legs
When she wanted a meal
And hide behind the sofa
When she felt ill
She would bring us a present
Of a bird or a mouse
Leave them on the doorstep
Or around the house
I didn't like it
But what could I do?
It was just her way of saying
That she loved me too!

Joan Taylor

An ode to Kipper (My cat)

My friend and ally, unbeknown,
Who *else* so feline would accept my home?
Creature comforts, all on tap,
With no problems, bills, ice or bats!

We had our troubles when we met,
For two months, strife ridden, and vet beset!
Then as time progressed, each with our ways,
We became so loyal and becrazed!

A snug little cuddle and a purr,
With a cold wet nose, they do not deter;
That boiling pot and pickling jar,
The threats that beset me, went so far!

And when she's sick and in a huddle and so forlorn,
Her bright eyes gone, full of misery, denying food and all interest in life,
If tender loving care and a gentle cuddle do not suffice,
Then it's down to the vet, in a trice!

Rosemary E Pearson

Millie's Manoeuvres

Energy fast and furious
Into the leaves she went,
One little terrier full of enthusiasm,
Enjoying freedom was the immediate intent.

As gentle breezes descended
Swirling amongst undergrowth,
Excitement was evidently seen
When four paws pounced with delight.

Snuffling, barking, what did she see?
An imaginary bone, or reality?
She appeared to be in earnest, her tail wagging fast.
Was it worth the effort? Had she found it at last?

Shaking and quaking with anticipation,
In reverse gear she hauled it out.
A plastic bone with bells inside.
She proudly presented the item, to echoes of doggy shouts.

Have we searched for something elusive?
Diligently sought with zeal?
It's very important to find Him.
God, through Jesus revealed.

Our eternal future is very exciting,
Happiness for evermore.
Present ourselves before the only One
Who can cleanse and make us whole.

Shout and sing from the rooftop.
Be diligent in searching God's word
The Father on high is observing
Every action His subjects perform.

Annie R Harcus

My Cat, Tootsie

Now you're gone
Oh how I wish you were here
Here still with me
With me you were my best friend
The best friend I ever had
Tootsie you knew when I was upset or tired
But still you were there
There for me
I miss your sweet face
I miss you sat next to me
One day I see you
See you in Heaven
Heaven I can't wait
Wait for that day
The day I'll be with you
You are now free from the pain
Pain you won't have no more
Oh how I wish you were here
Here still with me
With me the best friend I ever had
Ever had and that is you.

Angela Cole

Twig

Her name is Twiggy and when she arrived
She was small and slim, we thought *will she survive?*
You could tell at a glance, she's an aristocrat
And came from good stock, an intelligent cat
When you enter the house to pay a call
Her stare says plainly, you're not welcome at all
I'll just stay awhile, now that you're here
Then very quietly I'll disappear
Most antisocial you can read her thoughts
Then with a sweep of her tail, off she walks
There's a box in the hall which she rarely uses
Thinks: well bred cats prefer private bushes
If you think that I shall sit on that
You can think again, I'm a dignified cat
Enjoying a prowl at dead of night
Even the foxes take their flight
If you enter the bedroom, you'll find her asleep
Tucked up in a blanket on top of the sheet
The birds have decided to take it in turns
To keep a look out as they search for worms
And are careful to note as they take a bath
That Twiggy's not coming down the path
Of the cats next door I must just say
She's not too pleased they're here to stay
When she sits on the wall with her stony stare
They know that they had better beware
Seems they would like to be friends, but there playing it cool
Take matters slow they're not ones to be fooled
So that's our Twig, a cat with a character
What I've said is all true, you'll see if you meet her
Her shiny black coat has a beautiful sheen
And eyes of green that are sharp and keen
With all the care she gets each day
She'll perhaps live for ever, well years anyway

Phyllis Dawson

My Mum

My mum is OK
She does her best to please
I like her chicken dinners
But she won't let me have cheese
My mum is OK
I take her out for walks
But if she meets one of her friends
She talks and talks!
My mum is OK
She's really very good
I've spent a long time training her
To do just as she should
She doesn't always get it right
Sometimes I have to scold
But if I look her in the eye
She'll do as she is told
My mum is OK
She shares my double bed
She drives the car, I navigate
She does the shopping and I wait
She gives me a bath
And that I *hate!*
But I love her all the same
My mum is OK.

Ben Livesey (1994-2006)

Raining Cats And Dogs

It was, I thought, a metaphor
that talked of cats and dogs,
in terms of falling like the rain
in spoken dialogue.

Yet while out walking yesterday
the queerest thing took place.
'Twas dogs and cats indeed that did
rebound from off my face.

Oh yes! 'Twas raining cats and dogs
I know you've heard it said,
but truly several ginger toms
did strike me on my head.

And as I howled then craned my neck
to gaze up at the sky.
A bulldog, then an Afghan hound
did strike me on each eye.

'Twas at that point I threw up arms
and cried out, 'What the heck?'
But scarcely had I closed my lips
as two shih-tzus struck my neck.

The next thing I remember then
was waking up in bed.
A hospital! That's where I was!
They'd patched and stitched my head.

So now whenever raindrops fall
I keep a watchful eye,
for furry things like dogs and cats
a-tumbling from the sky.

Daniel Barnett

Let Me In

I hear you, I am coming,
Don't shake your fur that way,
You had better stay,
I don't know why you get,
Put out every night,
You gave me a fright,
Standing by the light,
Drink your milk and we,
Will get to bed, we are both,
Sleepy heads.
Now we will be safe in the night,
'Til morning comes and it gets light.

Beryl Elizabeth Moore

Billy The Cat

Billy the tabby
was fast becoming Billy the tubby!
Billy protested.
He was comfortable with that,
he liked being fat.

It was decided to put him on a diet.
Billy decided to start a riot!
Took to smoking, staying out late and heavy drink,
the family had to quickly rethink
the situation, were not best pleased
with such insubordination.
Everyone was appalled,
a family meeting was called.
They would reverse their decision
on the condition
he would watch his weight,
give up smoking, drinking, stopping out late -
and attend AA meetings.

Billy the tabby
happy to be a tabby
coughs up his regards
and sends his warmest greetings.

Martin Conway

Pet Stray Resting

I am not all I seem, a soft touch,
Melting at your call and warm
Fingers. Often enough
I've slept rough; yet my kind
Was once thought divine
Long before humans reckoned time.
I sing for my supper since I choose,
Not through need. It suits
I can fend for myself when I must.
Born killer, bred for hunting,
I excel at bloodshed and cunning,
My weapons of destruction sure -
Quilted flick-knives, fangs under fur.
My cross-bred coat's not common:
Its stripes of ochre and carbon
Ripple with an ancient beauty
That is nature's pedigree.

With caresses I sue for your hearth,
But your garden I rule outright,
Fleet-footed Angel of Death.

R Doman

Kiki

In the late afternoon on a day in July
A charming young lady came to stay
Clothed in white fur with a head so neat
Big blue eyes and such tiny feet
Sometimes she is naughty, scampers upstairs
Scatters my toys, hides under the chair
Climbs up the duvet, romps on the bed
Clings to my skirt as she waits to be fed
We rarely scold her so enchanting is she
For she's still just a baby, our kitten Kiki.

Doreen Goodway

Humphrey

Humphrey the cat is a very fine cat
For Humphrey knows just where he's at
Ten Downing Street no less than that.

He guards the papers of the realm
Inspects where heads of state will dwell
And sniffs out trouble where he can.

He even has his photo fans
In Downing Street there's none so grand
He also claims his special perks
Like ducklings from Saint James' Park.

For Blairs may come and Blairs may go
But here's a fact that he does know:
Humphrey the cat will always stand
As premier mouser in the land.

Oh dear, we hear that's not quite true
Our hero passed to glories new
Another mouser fills his space
And very grandly sniffs the place.

A glamour puss of feline charm
Who rules the realm with cunning calm
And prowls around to mice alarm
Then postures, purrs to media balm.

Her name is Sybil, if you will
Who licks her lips at all she'll kill
And proudly guards Ten Downing's chief
Which should give Gordon much relief.

Rosemary Keith

Oh Not Again

The lead, oh not again,
Doesn't she know it's going to rain?
My fur gets wet, my feet are cold,
I do not want to go for a walk,
She'll only stop and stand and talk.
It'll be the park, the shops, or river
And I expect I'll just stand and shiver.
I'd rather lie beside the fire,
It's too much to expect of me.
I'm much to old now, can't she see,
My paws feel sore, my back just aches,
And when it's cold I get the shakes.
But no, it's walkies time again,
Through the sun, snow or rain.
If I could speak, I'd let her know
This walkies business has got to go,
Just leave me here to lie and sleep,
Let her go out, all on her own
While I stay here and wait, at home.

Hazel Webb

Dog's Best Friend

You brought me home to live.
I'm grateful for that day.
If given speaking skills,
I would benignly say -

O' thank you for the walks
and all the doggy grubs.
My floppy ears enjoy
the daily tender rubs.

I crave your body scent,
with or without cologne.
I seek it in your clothes
when I am left alone.

My role I hold with pride.
Security's my job.
I'm also glad to bring
the laughter when you sob.

I understand your moods,
adopting them as mine.
Instincts reveal to me
when everything is fine.

At times I feel forlorn
when others beckon you.
My loyalty remains,
for you adore me too.

I've never won a show.
No mantel flaunts a prize.
I seek a high reward:
approval in your eyes.

Nanette Orange

Horatio

Our grandchild is a hamster named Horatio,
Our daughter's Shakespeare mad as you'll have guessed,
As all my friends are proud of their grandchildren,
So we think our Horatio's the best.

A very friendly soul is our Horatio,
He sleeps all day and wakes up of a night,
And if you stick your finger near his cake 'ole,
He can't half give your finger end a bite!

All my friends' grandchildren are small humans,
But they are nothing near to so much fun,
Cos they can't put their grandkids in a plastic ball,
And stick 'em on the floor and watch 'em run.

Mick Nash

Who's Looking At Who?

The light shines brightly above
The three drifters adorned in gold
As they arrive at an enchanted castle.
Nobody answers the door.
Grey, covered in moss; it's deserted.
Two large towers loom over them;
Quietness, stillness, wetness.
What can it mean?
The surge from a large water pump
Is still active but nobody's here.
Why has everybody left?
In search of the truth they travel
Through a thick elevated green forest.
Slowly they emerge
Arriving at an old stone bridge;
Part of the wall now missing.
They wonder where it can lead?
Afraid to cross above, exposed,
They glide underneath the arch
Silently examining all areas of it.
The ground here, a carpet of gravel,
Leads to an assortment of shells
Large and mysteriously placed.
Maybe a seashore?
They rise up to survey the scene ahead;
What lies beyond?
They're suddenly startled back,
Confronted by vast staring eyes,
As my husband and I peer
Through the crystal-clear wall
Of the tank that sits on our coffee table.

Rita Carter-Forde

Flower

These days I'm often feeling low, I do not have a lover
and I've a father I've never known.
But I always have Flower even when I pretend.
Away at university or staying at a friend's,
if I close my eyes I can still think of him then.
The smartest of all creatures, the most seductive smile -
he never moves his lips but I know he loves me all the while.
When I come home from work and there's no one else there,
he's always saying hello just by being there.
He never lets me down, all he wants is love, and since I'm so lacking
in that department I'm fond of giving him hugs.
It scares me how much I love him, miss him all the time,
if something ever happened I know I'd lose my mind.
But, that is why I make the most of each and every day,
whenever I see his little face he takes my pain away.
You see they never do you wrong, a cat can't bite or bark,
all they want is your attention and then they'll give it to you right back.
The best thing is you don't approach them; they're not waiting by the door like some
desperate thing.
You have to gain their trust, have to let them in.
Because it's when you're not acting needy,
that's when their love will show.
Independent, proud and chic, my Flower's always there for me -
the most amazing thing.
I love it when he climbs on me, just after when I bathe,
purring, pining, loving, he loves the scent of rose.
I take pictures all the time, so I'll remember who he is,
the kindest loving alarm clock that prowls around the woods.
So tonight he'll sleep next to me and I'll hear him purr,
but if he doesn't want to be there, he won't lie - he'll be out the door.
So I guess that's the reason why I love my baby so,
'cause even though he doesn't have to stay with me he always
comes back for more.
My sister picked his name and at first we all just laughed,
but now my baby Flower has ended up my other half.

Steven Murray

Chicki And Me

He's a pal,
And lets it show,
And I'm ashamed to say,
Those other cats know.
I met him young,
A ball of feathers,
Suspicion gave way,
To hours of pleasure.
He keeps a watch,
His patience bold,
The law of the jungle,
Put on hold.
We stroll around,
A very odd couple,
Always alert,
Avoiding trouble.
He dive bombs my path,
My stride to measure,
I swipe a paw,
In token gesture.
Outside the window,
I hear a titter,
Those other cats,
Have come to litter.
My street-cred gone,
I hide in shame,
It's my feathered friend,
Who's all to blame.

Stephen Humphries

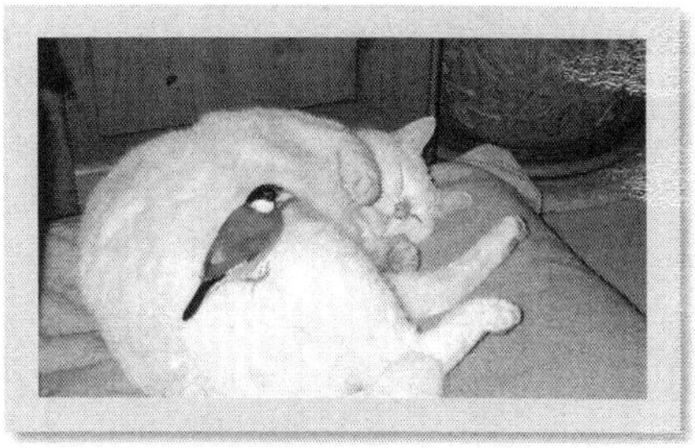

Puppies, Puddles And Pebbles

My new pup whizzes everywhere
Nose to the ground, leg in the air.
Lamp post, chair or garden gate
I try to stop him, oops too late!
Pink twitching nose busily scents the air,
Sniffing and whizzing without a care.
I expect he does it to leave his mark,
With wagging tail and high-pitched bark.
His toasty breath and python teeth,
He licks my toes and tugs his leash.
My pup does it over his favourite tree
Does it once and then
Two minutes up the road,
He's at it again.
When he feels the urge to go,
He waters pot plants and melts the snow.
His chubby leg cocked up high,
It's embarrassing when he sprinkles passers-by.
With newspaper, puppy tray at the ready
Clearing up can be a chore,
I try training him but he gets excited
Leaving little 'accidents' on the kitchen floor.

Amelia Michael

Fluffy

Oh! Fluffy how I love you,
God bless your little heart.
You pounce and leap upon everyone,
Your antics never seem to part,
You clamber upon our curtains,
Then come on running down
And when Mummy gets cross,
Hide 'neath my dressing gown.

You run so fast I gasp for breath,
In haste - I follow your trail.
Pulling along Mummy's knitting,
Now knotted around your tail.

Oh! Fluffy, please behave yourself,
Or Mummy shall throw you out.
I know you're only a kitten,
But you spread chaos all about.

I saw you eat Daddy's dinner
Though yours was there last night,
Then you chased a little field mouse
Which gave my mummy a fright.
Oh! Fluffy, I so adore you,
But like me - you must behave.
I think Fluffy heard my whisper,
Being so obedient and brave.

Fluffy now grey and old,
Purrs for love just the same.
No antics lovingly seen anymore,
But through memory is just as game.

S Kettlewell

I've Been Petted

If it hadn't been for Her
I wouldn't have had a pet.
But She loves them
And I can't deny Her anything.
So now I have the lot,
Canine, feline and equine,
But I swear I'll draw the line at porcine.

Naively, I imagined a dog, a Lab perhaps,
Lying on a rug before the fireplace,
Not on the couch between us.
Horses running free in the pasture,
Not filling their stalls with tons of waste
Per year (and that's a lot of pounds per day).
Little kitty with upturned face and adoration in her eyes,
Not yowling for the soft, canned food instead of the pelleted stuff.

Before they came, I imagined the love
Between dog and master, cat and mistress,
Even horse and rider.
But it's all about food; show any of them food
And they'll follow you anywhere.

And so these three abide:
Food, waste removal, and a warm place to stay.
But the greatest of these is food.

H Frank Gibbard

For The Love of Bonnie, The Cat

(Dedicated to my brother Bill Mooney and his good wife Susan and Bonnie their cat, with love)

Bonnie, for the love of elegance, to Susan,
The tabby cat, slides across the highly polished,
Brown floor: her beautiful, lame leg, outstretched,
Eight years ago, hit by a fast car, yet survived:
She, gliding in grace, upon her wonderful
Reflection, the tabby waltzes toward
The armchair of Susan, for the love of Bonnie.

Edmund Saint George Mooney

Sam

Gone to where again? Wearing out trainers
at the school of wag. That dog just won't learn.
Bought from Harpurhey home for a fiver
and slept by the growling fire a week
when not finding ways through doors
and garden hedges. Turning up in the ginnel
after a week away, sheltering from the rain.

John Cox

Thank God!

I am the only female in a house that's full of males,
but the one who is the best behaved is the male that owns a tail.

He comes when I call, he sits when I ask, and never answers back,
I really wish they were all like him, cos the others need the sack.

He cannot leave the seat up when he has to go the loo,
and leave the bath towels on the floor, or wipe the sink, not much to do.

He doesn't leave his things around, or his trainers in the hall,
the only thing that he's allowed is his soft and squeaky ball.

He doesn't ask me questions when my favourite programme's on,
he lies with me, so quietly, and I'm never put upon.

He doesn't leave his dishes lying dirty on the side,
and when he's asked to do something; he doesn't go and hide.

No! Smudge is loyal and giving, and we enjoy our daily jog,
so I love him and look after him, and thank God that he's a dog!

Gaynor Latham-Chadwick

Alfie's Habits

Stop!

I've had enough.
It's always don't
do this, don't do that.
I want to lay on
the bed, chew off a
doll's head. I want
to play in the park
and they say shhhhs
when I want to bark.
It's just not fair.
Oh and if I could I'd
attack a doll's hair.

Carla Leek

Pussy's Prayer

O Lord of four-legged creatures
I purr my feline prayer -
My grateful thanks for shelter
And food beyond compare.
And for my two legg'd servant
Who tends me night and day,
Who opens doors and grooms me well -
For her kind heart I pray.
She cannot climb as I can
Nor jump and things like that,
So grateful thanks for seeing
That I'm your wonder cat.
Then for all other felines
When life is hard this day,
And for all strays and ferals
Be with them Lord, I pray.
So now I'll close my eyes to muse
How wonderful to be
Just as you made me Lord - a cat
And not a human *she*.

Owen Edwards

Red Brick Epitaph

The first I knew of it was his noise, which was no more than a small cry.
It was all he dared;
And not even that when she released him - for he knew her plan.

Wet from her spit, he shook his head
Raised proudly even so,
Although he knew his fate.
I watched him at the kitchen doorway, and I was the coward.

When she came for him again he did not move,
But once again, that cry!

Was he so far from home?
Who knows if his mate heard, if nestlings stirred, mewled?
Yet I returned the call, and I gave chase.

She clamped her jaws, defiant;
I knew his bones would break,
And yet my hands were gentle with her mouth - each lover to her love!

Her kittenhood, not his, was my restraint;
Her life the one I'd known.
Was I so partisan? So nepotist? So wrong?

The third time, and the fourth, she let him stand transfixed,
Until I came between them, trembling myself with rage.

And when I did, it was not to restore him to his grassy nest,
His fingernail-sized brood, his unknown life
A dozen yards from mine.

With mind averted, clamped, I raised my brick
And let it fall.

His cries were done - not mine!
The kitten washed her face; I went to weep.
Her mouth had been the trap; my brick the instrument.
Both natures stained with blood - but mine not innocent.

Tricia Booth

Swapping

Her head rests on the edge of the bed
Returning her love, showing highbred.
Comfortable life in this new home
No more farm days to roam all alone.

Spotty dog of exceptional breed
Said work on the farm, there is no need.
Out in all weathers, rounding up sheep
Remembering those times just made her weep.

Katy and Spotty had been mismatched
With heads together, their plan, they hatched.
Our Katy would be taking control
By destroying her mistress' soul.

Everything tried, the last straw came
When Katy bit again and again!
Now they had done the dastardly deed
And swapped places, both now freed.

Miss Mary

Tigg

I used to have lots of greyhound mates,
Together we would race and chase,
Until I could no longer keep up the pace.

Suddenly I was all alone
I sniffed and walked,
But found no one I'd known.
I cried and whined,
All on my own.

The cold, dusty pavements were my bed,
The damp, dirty dustbins were my dinner,
And all because I was no longer a winner.

Then a guardian angel came my way,
Her name is Debs Rothary.
She made me welcome at a place called Tia,
Along you came and found me here.

You all had so much love to give,
It brought back my strength and will to live.
Now I'm content, think I've found gold,
Happy to know my story's been told.

Rachel Sutcliffe

Susie

She's such a little character
And full of mischief too
Her coat is black and shiny
She watches what I do

The house is full of life now
You always know she's there
I bless the day I had my cat
So wonderful and rare.

Susan Bamford

Ode To A Perfect Landlady

I used to love my partner,
We got on really well
until another caught his eye
and my life became hell.

I'd wait and watch on the corner,
eternally faithful and true,
but he'd stop out for supper and breakfast as well,
I decided to find pastures new.

I spotted this kind-looking person,
who resides just two doors down the lane,
so I put on my lean and hungry look,
and acted like I was in pain.

My tactics could not have worked sooner,
hook, line and sinker she fell,
she served me a morsel of tuna
and I knew she was under my spell.

I'm in love with my landlady,
she's an angel in disguise,
she caters for my every need
when I roll my big green eyes.

I'm in love with my landlady,
she treats me like a king,
it's a pity she's fifty years older than me
and wears a wedding ring.

I'm in love with my landlady,
It don't matter I'm black and she's white,
Colour prejudice isn't an issue with us,
and I sleep in her bed every night.

Mavis Worrall

My Pony

There once was a pony that would stand by her gate,
And wait for me even when I was late.
I would offer her a carrot, an apple or two,
Pick her feet, check her shoe.

Tacked up, ready to go,
A fast hack or shall we go slow?
My pony seemed to tell me the answer,
Prancing and dancing just like a dancer.

Along the lane, up a track,
Getting faster, oh what a hack!
Galloping quickly, having fun!
My pony is definitely my number one!

Walking slowly, thinking back,
I don't think I've ever had a bad hack.
Loving my pony isn't a test,
As I know my pony is the best.

Emma Massey

My Kitten Called Rainbow

I have a little kitten
Rainbow is her name
She is always full of mischief
She is driving me insane!
She scurries up the curtains
And swings right from the top
She always knocks things over
I wonder if it will ever stop
She's broken lots of ornaments
Some were very dear to my heart
But I just love her oh so much
Our lives will never part . . .
She loves to cuddle up at night
Beside my big toy tiger
I think it makes her feel at home
With the great big cat beside her . . .
She's a gorgeous little kitty
Her fur is white as snow
She's so full of fun, she's crazy
I think that's why I love her so . . .
When she jumps into the fish pond
Her coat turns shades of green
If she brushes past some yellow paint
She's the most colourful cat I've seen
I've seen her streaks of violet
Red and orange, blue and indigo
I think I chose the perfect name for her
My precious little kitten called Rainbow!

Janet Brook

Bobby

Here is a tale of the dog I own
I remember the day when I brought him home,
Such a tiny little bundle
Nervous and shy
By looking at him now you'd never see why.

When I first laid eyes on my tiny pup
And saw those big brown eyes look straight up
I knew I couldn't abandon such a delight
So brought him home that very night.

I gave a name to him from me
And from that day on he was known as Bobby.
I learnt from him as he learnt from me
We are an inseparable pair now known as we.

It's been seven years now
And he's still by my side,
Loyal as ever
He fills me with pride.

It's those eyes still that bring him attention and care
And those eyes do I see under his scruffy hair.
All ruffled and rugged yet cute and full of need,
My Yorkie is such a wonderful breed.

He brings me happiness,
Love and joy,
Although he's sometimes a nuisance
He is a good boy.

He's lazy in the evenings
Laying on the sofa each night,
But when morning comes he's a bouncing delight.
Sticking his little nose here and there
That's when you see it peeking out from his hair!

Victoria Sloan

Heavenly Mystery

Now chasing rabbits is all very well
And plenty of fun I'm sure,
But dropping your tennis balls down their burrows
Is getting a bit of a bore.
That's three yellow Dunlops you've sent down there
With never a thought of the cost.
And what do you think it's going to achieve
Now they're irretrievably lost.
And heaven knows what the rabbit will think
Deep in its earthy hole.
It will certainly have a lot to say
To its close neighbour, the mole.

'Did you know the sun fell down from the sky
And landed on my head.
And then again the following day
While I was still in bed.
And blow me down if two minutes later
It went and happened once more.
And here's me thinking there's only one sun,
It's breeding like rabbits galore!'

Jinny Casey

Compromise

I met a bird with vertigo
whose progress up was rather slow.
I asked, why not stay upon the ground?
What with all those cats around,
you must think I am rather thick
to fall for that old silly trick.
So now to my extreme surprise
we have reached a compromise
like politicians in a sense,
he spends his time upon the fence.

P Colenutt

The Gentle Persuader

He looked at me and smiled,
I didn't care.
Then he rubbed his chin upon my knee
Giving his softest stare.
The faintest sigh escaped his lips,
Soft hair brushed my skin.
I turned my head the other way
As I felt myself give in.
His golden eyes persuaded me
To break my solemn vow
Not to feed that rotten cat again.
So here I am right now
Chopping him some dainty meat
Ensnared by his miaow . . .

S Nicolaou

Connor - The Human Cat!

(Dedicated to my friends Connor and Caroline Guy)

He follows his mistress wherever she goes.
Well known at the corner shop.
He comes in and curls up on my sofa
Quite at home
Like a good neighbour.
He's a very handsome fellow
He knows he is 'Top Cat'
Of the neighbourhood.
Always preening his fine whiskers
Or shining coat,
Always stops to say 'Howdy'
In his own way!
You can't ignore this creature
For he escorts me in the garden
Or dozes on the shed roof
One eye open.
He won't miss a trick!

Liz Osmond

Only A Puppy Dog That Wagged His Tail

Only a puppy dog that wagged his tail
Who jumped into your arms, he could not fail
You took him home, the children all loved him
He chewed up your slippers, jumped on the bed
When chastised he sat then tilted his head
How could you ever not forgive him?
Grew big and strong, obeyed every command
Lay at your feet, loved the stroke of your hand
Played with the children until they were grown
Fetched sticks from the river, shook himself dry
Laughing and screaming the children would fly
Lies at your feet now the children have flown
Still barks at the cat, smells food from a mile
His life span is short you reflect for a while
You remember the last walk to the vet
The injection that released him from pain
He will never walk at your side again
Tears fill your eyes, he was more than a pet.

David M Walford

Let Me Belong

'Clear off,' was all he ever heard, thrown in with the usual swear word;
Where did he clear off too? What was he to do?
No one ever said 'go to here or there',
He had no way of knowing, where he was to go:
Which direction was the zone of 'Come on in?'
For he knew that place, he'd never been, why was it so hard to find,
Had he done wrong, had he sinned, then why was he always to blame?
He was tired, weary of age and pain, from being kicked,
If he hadn't moved quick,
As someone growled, 'Clear off, or you'll get this stick.'
Many times, these sticks came down upon his back.

He hadn't bothered anyone, just took an old bone, partly picked,
It lay alongside, a yard bin, thrown away, the dust cart would have gone over it, next day.

He drank from gutter water, whenever there was rain,
Sometimes, when the sun was high, lips so dry, he'd pull at grass
Along the kerb, if not he would have died.

'Clear off,' the familiar cry, echoed in his head,
He couldn't rest a moment, before those words were said.

Winter, this year, was to be the end for him, he knew;
If that is it, let it be so, he resigned himself, to death;
He would lie alongside the wall, where he knew caught the flurries of snow.

It came that night, no further he could go, the snow would cover him, Like a woollen
blanket and no one would know where he lay
And when uncovered, how long had been the stay;
He closed his eyes to the cold, that swept along with the snow
And sank into the drift, no more to know.

The dream is so real, where was this place, the snow woollen
Blanket, the cold he had felt, was gone;

'There old man, soon have you well.'
Other words than 'Clear off', it must have a better meaning,
Though even if a dream, he could tell.
A basket for his bed, a pillow at his head, a plate beside him,
With a wondrous assortment, that had ever met his eyes;

If he closed his eyes, tight shut, would it be, he would wake up;
We think not, for love has come his way, at last, no more
Cold, or, 'Clear offs' and 'Clear aways',
But warmth, for all his days.

L Hammond oberansky

Chester And Soli

The garden fence fell down today,
Not solely caused by wind and rain;
With thirteen pounds of former stray,
The trellis couldn't stand the strain.

When Chester climbs the yucca tree,
It wobbles like an old man's knees,
And when he stands aloft I see,
His belly flapping in the breeze.

His brother hunts without remorse,
Not using sleight of hand (or paws),
For Soli, there's another course:
Awaiting bird with open jaws.

You may expect me now to write,
Like Blake, of tigers, burning bright,
Though I must say that of a night,
They're more like tree sloths, sleeping tight.

Catherine osborn

A Hole In our Lives Now You Are Gone

(For Mousey 1995-2007)

God bless her little feline soul
In all our hearts she has left a hole
We miss her gentle loving ways
A cuddle at the end of busy days
She was timid, meek and mild
My older little feline child
When she came to me from the rescue place
I admired her wise and beautiful face
Her oriental beauty enthralled us all
But for a week she wouldn't answer our call
She had been beaten and hurt and didn't want more
So from under my bed I would hear her snore
A week later emerged this beautiful beast
She settled down to a veritable feast
She received attention and cuddles and love
Now we commend her to you above
For ten wonderful years she had our love
God bless her little beautiful soul
For in all our hearts she has left a hole.

Derek Blackburn

Debbie And Sally

One black, one nearly white
Two little dogs, one summer night
In fun and fancy free
Scampered off with glee
Over the rockery wall they leapt
No ear at all
For their master's call
On to the scent of a mole
Debbie, Sally came rasping
In the still summer evening
And the sound of a thrush
In a nearby bush
The road to be crossed
And soon to be lost
To sight, and in the field
The wheeled ruts and the mud congealed
To ford the running water
Where perhaps an otter
Has its lair. That was a fox
They are trying now to coax
A rabbit from its burrow
Which wisely waits tomorrow
Now the dew is falling
There is still someone calling
But it was fun
To leave the house and run.

Elizabeth Love

Trooper And Me

To the field, Trooper and me run,
Play fetch ball, just for the fun,
Lots of brollies to block the sun.
Waving at Trooper, with my hand,
He just chases the birds that try to land,
He's panting heavily, running on the grassland.
Me and my dog were up at sunlight,
He wants to stay, but I have to write,
Come on Trooper, it's nearly twilight.
I shout his name, he runs towards me,
I hear his footsteps, very faintly,
I can't see him, oh he's only a puppy.
I turn around, there he sits,
I shout him over and give him some doggy bits,
I ruffle his fur and put on my mitts.
I start to walk and Trooper follows,
Where are we going? Trooper knows.

Alisha Harbach

Poem About Spike

His colours shine
iridescent gold and green
coal-black eyes
diamond-bright
face soft as cloud
head bent
begging love

soon, my fingertips buried
and where they weave
muted grumbles and half hellos
silken and rustling
as I stop
pools of down close
to fledgling surprise
and indignant squeals

sometimes
he plays
hawk-rough
head bobbing
like a back-seat dog
clothes and skin
prized and torn
my lap
his auditorium
his wrecking yard

and there
in consent
tip-clawed shock
or musty, cotton-ball sleep
his playground
his asylum
his throne

Carolyn Edwards

The old Farmer And His Collie

No more will we hear his familiar bark
No more looking to him after dark
Poor Bruce's life finished a hard way
He had to be put to sleep on Christmas Day

When he had the farm he fetched the cows each day
He never received anything in pay
Up and down the hills his coat blowing in the wind
A better cow dog you could not find

Thunder and lightning and fireworks he could not bear
He used to come in the house and lie beside me in the chair
Now his shed is empty and his lead hangs loose
I have to go walkies without dear old Bruce

At sixteen and a half years he was an old timer
But as a dog there was none any finer
Just one injection in the vein
And poor old Bruce was free from pain

R J Moulton

The Lonely Angel

An angel was lonely in Heaven,
She wanted a pet of her own.
She looked down to my garden and saw you,
And noticed how old you had grown.
She'd watched you since you were a puppy,
She'd laughed at your antics and games.
She protected you when there was danger,
Now she wants to protect you again.

The time now came for her to take you
To her home, way out past the moon.
For her, the timing was perfect and right,
But for me, it was much, much too soon.
For you were my friend and companion,
You were with me through good times and bad.
And as I look back through my memories,
I'm so glad for the times that we had.

She came down as you lay, quietly sleeping,
Put her arms round you, held you so near.
She whispered your name, and you answered,
But your leaving has left me in tears.
She took you far over the rainbow,
On paths made by the sun's golden rays.
To a land full of green fields and flowers,
Where again, you relive puppy days.

Every night as I look up to Heaven,
I see stars that are twinkling so bright.
And I seem to know that you are watching,
Keeping me safe through the night.
But each night that goes by brings me closer
To the time my life's finally through.
When that angel comes down to collect me,
And takes me up to Heaven and you.

Maggie Moore

Ain't Life Grand

Mum's putting some bread in a carrier bag,
Woof, woof, tail wag hooray,
It means I'm off to the park again,
I've already been once today.

We're going to feed the ducks, geese and swans,
But these birds don't care much for me,
So while Dad chucks bread for their dinner,
I race round the park with glee.

Say hello to a friendly pal or two,
Have a nuzzle, a sniff, a few wees
Then back to my dad by the river,
Go content home to Mum for our tea.

Dream of tomorrow's adventures,
As I drift off to sleep, tummy full,
Such a lucky doggie, I know that,
So loved by my old dad and mum.

Dorothy M Mitchell

Paddy

Paddy wants to jump in for a swim
but our ducks refuse to let him in
They are happy to splash and have fun
upside down their tails in the sun
So Paddy decides to walk away
and try his luck another day

Valerie ovais

Trust

Children and dogs, should be raised in the same way.
Lots of love and discipline, from the first day.

Understanding and trust, to have faith in one another.
Care for your dog like some loved sister or brother.

It looks for your guidance, hangs on your every word.
Friendship in silence, good to be heard.

Not man and animal another species, a friend.
How sad that such dependency, some time has to come to an end.

T A Napper

Sally

Wistful pup in the wire pen, nervous and unsure,
What heartless person threw you out
And made you insecure?

I wonder did you have a name that you once answered to
It might well have been 'Goldie', for your coat is of that hue.

Your ribs stick out like barrel rungs, your rump has mountain peaks,
It's very plain you haven't had a decent meal in weeks.

No more to wander all alone or scavenge in some alley,
We'll take you home to love and feed,
And call you our pal Sally.

Cheryl Hier

Lines For A Husky Puppy Raised In Africa

In this unnatural place
for your kind
the thunder you hear
the wailing rain on the roof
will change in your mind
to the belief
that a glacier has calved
and a berg
has roared into the bay
and that the midnight wind
has left his sleeping place
to search for prey.

Your coat is dusky white
to deceive the eye
of the marauding bear -
your eyes are the bleached blue
of the snow-sky.
In your wisdom you know
that the trails in the dust
on our dirt road
are the tracks of a sleigh,
dog-hauled, with a light load
driven across the snow
to pass this way.

You can never belong
to our sun-world,
our soft-starred night -
always at the edge of winter
you are the reminder
of the departing light.
You know the sun
must put off his gold hood
one evening soon
and creep away -
then you will run and run

beside the master-hunter
over the frozen bay -
one of a dog-team
pulling a hunting sleigh
in the path of the moon.

Finola Holiday

Boris

What can I say? What can I do?
Every second of the day
I'm missing you!

I touch your collar, I shed a tear
I can't believe that you're not here
I see you waiting by your bowl
Your image fills my very soul

Devil dog Rottweiler they said of you
Everyone knows that this wasn't true
Beautiful Boris I'm missing you

Each day gets harder without you my friend
You were loving and gentle until the end
Grandchildren cried and friends did too
I never thought I could be this blue

Jock is pining and I am too
Always and forever
We'll be missing you

Rose Horscroft

Puppy John

Nell had got out of her kennel when she wasn't right
And some weeks later, one puppy was born in the night
Young Joe was pleased, having two dogs to have fun
But Nell was poorly after the birth, and could not run

Young Joe now realised that no longer would she bark
She was buried nearby, with a wooden cross as a mark
The boy's mother asked him to name the dog just born
'What the puppy? Well, I think John, the puppy, John'

'Unusual,' the mother said, 'we will call it Puppy John'
Over the next few months, the dog was as good as anyone
He was well trained, very intelligent, and almost as wise
Like herding stray cattle, helping lambs, such a good prize

He could swim and bark at the same time, just like a hound
And always protected young Joe, when danger was around
Other dogs kept out of its way, because this land was his
No trespassing by others was allowed, that was a promise

One day young Joe took Puppy John for some exercise
He chased rabbits, meaning them no harm, only to surprise
The boy and dog ran about, chasing each other in play
Joe jumped a fence, and as he landed the ground gave way

Down he went, into an old mine some distance from the top
Puppy John was barking on the edge, as Joe began to drop
He had been told of the mine, but thought that it was a joke
No joke now as he lay at the bottom with his leg broke

It seemed like hours, when Joe heard Puppy John bark
A rope and stretcher were lowered, as Joe lay in the dark
He was pulled to safety, and spent a day in a hospital bed
Puppy John was given a medallion for his collar, then fed

William A Laws

Stuffed Bunny

The torment begins as he hears the gates close - *whack*
He starts off at a sprint, no looking back
Twelve dogs behind catching up fast
Everything blurs as he runs quickly past

What a life for a rabbit always being chased
A rough reality in this dull smoky place
He has become stuck in this never-ending loop
All he wishes for now is to be shut in a coop

He looks behind, they're in a tight pack
Corner turned he keeps to the track
He is slowing now, can't keep up the pace
Thank goodness it's just a greyhound race!

Kirsty Little

Precious Love . . .

Seven pairs of eyes were watching me,
Though not one word was said.
They gathered to rub against me
As I patted every head.
Every once in a while
A cat would nudge my hand.
I then began my stroking,
Message clear, I understand.
One head would rub against my knees,
Another would nibble at my toes.
All done so soft, so tender,
With a love that grows and grows.
Am conscious of seven pairs of eyes
That kindly look to me.
I am contented with their friendship
And the trust that I can see.
Who could ask for anything more,
They have filled a lonely heart.
All they give is unconditional
With a bond that none can part.
When I arise, with hair a mess
To them it doesn't mean a thing.
They surround me with their affection,
Such a warmth to me they bring.
After years of being criticised
'Tis with joy I take their care.
God has taught me of true love.
Their eyes show it, every pair.
I trust them so, as they trust me
And we rest quietly by the fire.
I thank the Lord who has made it so,
He has given me my heart's desire.
Love.

Rosie Hues

Cats

They speed along at twenty miles per hour
Some cats only sit and contemplate
Some snuggle down in bed and have a catnap
Some are hand fed cos this is what they rate
Some cats take a pride in their appearance
Some cats only sit and watch the view
Some cats travel to far off places
And all of them when asked answer miaow!
Cats always come in many disguises
Many varieties of them you can expect
But each of them to someone is a treasure
You could say that they are all purr-fect.

Joyce Hudspith

An Ode To A Doggie

A dog is such a treasure,
Of your life becomes a part.
Before you even know it,
Has overruled your heart.

No matter how you're feeling,
He never lets you down.
Such a loving welcome,
With faithful eyes of brown.

But sadly they grow older,
And have to leave your side.
But memories are forever,
And with you will abide.

There is a doggie heaven
Up in the clear blue sky.
The love you gave stays with them,
So they never really die.

Peggy Howe

Charm's Bad Work

Lying in my bed feeling a little sad
Oh yes, I know that I've been bad
But what does she expect when we're left alone?
Just me and Granny here at home.

A little jump was all it took
To reach her knitting and pattern book
The stitches fell off one by one
And the big ball of wool gave us so much fun.

Up the stairs and round the table legs
It reached from the lounge right up to the beds
Some bits I chewed and some I left
When she saw what I'd one she was quite bereft!

Her first prize was gone in the twinkle of an eye
When I ate her two foot prickly cacti
Will I have hedgehogs instead of pups?
Imagine her sitting with those on her lap!

Then on Monday beneath her feet I got
She dropped the dinner - meat, veg, the lot
Oh doggy paws you should've heard the roar
When she saw the mess on her kitchen floor.

Why do these 'two legs' make such a fuss?
The answer really is so obvious
Just call my name and I'll run -
A vacuum, mop, rolled into one!

So it's off to training classes now for me
I'll get my diploma just wait and see
Two hours of lessons - for her advice
Oh how to lead a less stressful life!

Anne Haynes

Biffy

We walked into the entrance hall -
Wondering which to take, and what to call
The ginger, oyster, black or white
And then we saw this tiny sight
At the stairhead.

This ball of fluff so very small
Raced down the stairs and round the hall,
Dashed up the stairs, ten times his size,
And stared at us with cheeky eyes
From the stairhead.

Long-haired, white, and black, and grey,
With a cheeky face and full of play.
We took him home 'fore we'd thought it out -
Rather, he chose us - without a doubt!
From the stairhead.

We took him home, this tiny mite,
Cowered and quiet, and lacking fight.
But within a day he was at full strength,
'Biffing' about to his heart's content!
We called him Biff!

And seven years later he was still the same -
'Biff' by nature and 'Biff' by name.
Hurtling about all over the place,
In character with the feline race!
Was Biff.

Sadly, he passed at the age of eight
After an illness which sealed his fate.
There was nothing at all anyone could do
And in his sad little face, he knew this too.
Did Biff.

Beautifully natured and easy to please,
A pampered mog with a life of ease.
He ruled the house - most decidedly!
But for the pleasure he brought, we wouldn't have been
Without Biff.

Val Hall

Wood Green Shelter

W here are animals cared for to brighten up their day?
O ut in the open countryside, to eat and rest and play.
O ne special place is Wood Green, a shelter for our friends,
D oing lots of loving things, a home where searching ends.

G uidance they will give you, support that you can see,
R eally giving all their time, to show how love comes free.
E ach animal is wanted no matter what their breed,
E very aspect to their way of life is given for their need.
N o funding they are blessed with at Wood Green Shelter Home,

S o they rely on charity to stop these animals' roam.
H elping is their motto to give these pets a place,
E ach member of the staff work hard with a smile upon their face.
L eaving pets and being cruel is such a wicked deed,
T o leave an animal starving or give the love they need.
E ach living thing has feelings; it's true some folk don't care,
R emember that your pets are friends don't forget that they are there.

Betty Hattersley

In Memory of Dennis

Sadly we miss you
We see your empty hutch
You were only a little bunny
And you didn't ask for much

Never any trouble
A gentle little chap
Always liked a cuddle
Or sit quietly on your lap

Goodbye little Dennis
We enjoyed your stay
We will not forget you
And we think of you today

Phyllis Hall

My Daughter's Dog

My daughter's dog called Trudie,
A black Cairn terrier, turning silver-grey,
She is an opportunist and often runs away,
And what with one thing and another.
For instance, she seems to think that I'm her mother,
I thought she needed therapy.
So I took her down to the university
To see the Professor of Scampology,
(Used to be a veterinary) and said to him,
'Test this dog and test her good,'
And he very kindly said he would.
So I went back the next day
Just to see what he had got to say,
He said, 'This dog's an opportunist
And she'll often run away,
But do not worry on that score,
For she'll always return to you again,
Because your image is imprinted on her brain,
And all her passions have been tested,
And I'm surprised she's not been arrested,
But all this passion's just for you
And all our tests prove this is true.'
So I said to the Professor of Scampology,
'Well, what does all this mean for me?'
And he said, 'It means she's your entire responsibility,
The only other thing I have to say
Is that there's rascality in her DNA.'

Stewart Gordon

our Embarrassing Pet

I visited a lady when I was on my bakery rounds,
She sold me a budgerigar it only cost five pounds,
Of course his name was Joey, he was blue and grey,
When he felt like talking you could understand what he did say,
'Georgie Porgie pudding and pie, kissed the girls and made them cry,'
He could recite quite as easily it seemed as you and I,
I taught him to say his name and address so,
If he flew away people would know where to return him to,
Unfortunately I did not know that Joey had heard,
Someone using an embarrassing short swear word,
The vicar visited me one night when I was very ill,
Joey was in his cage in the room sitting very still,
But when the vicar arrived and began to speak,
Joey shook his little head and opened wide his beak,
He really made me feel such a silly sort of pup,
When he shouted out, 'Will you B***** well shut up!'
The vicar looked amazed and really went quite red,
Picked up his hat, said goodnight and went home to bed.

Stan Gilbert

What's In A Name?

When our mum took us into her home,
We would never answer to our names,
So she set about re-naming us,
Third day our new names came.

New home, new life, is what she said,
So we answered immediately to her call,
We really like our new names,
The old ones didn't suit us all.

Corkey is our mum's other dog,
My name Rockey, is his jumbled up,
Ole pronounced Ollie is my brother's,
That came fro Leo, another Lhasa Mum had and loved.

To Mum and us our names are special,
Leo was the first true Lhasa she had,
Corkey came after Leo,
But unlike Leo, he'll never be a dad.

Mum told us how much she loved Leo,
We both know how much she loves Corkey too,
Mum says we are just as special,
So having their names makes us happy, never blue.

Mum loves all her animals dearly,
We're all treated exactly the same,
She never favours one above the other,
So glad to this home we came.

Gillian S Gill

Smurf

When I was just a youngster,
I would run and play all day,
I'd run and scamper, chasing
Leaves and birds and rabbits;
Once or twice I caught a mole!

As the years rolled slowly by,
I chased the birds and rabbits less,
But leaves and stones were still pursued,
With fun and games still the order of the day,
Also long walks that kept me fit.

Now I am much older,
So need the exercise more,
Still love my food you see!
But I am panking up this hill
Struggling like a good 'un.

Feeling rather tired.
A nice long rest when I get home.
Upon the couch, they won't mind.
After all, I'm their best mate,
Their ever faithful hound called Smurf!

Therese G Gilbert

Rescue Dogs

The St Bernard carries a brandy flask,
For travellers in distress.
The sniffer dog goes with eager nose,
Where humans can only guess,
The presence of naughty substances,
He finds 'em nonetheless!

A *greyhound* runs to the punter's song,
While show dogs pace the tent.
They say these days the foxhound bays,
To a softer sort of scent.
There'd be no risk of a brush with the law,
If the hunter upped and went.

Will a lap dog willingly go for a run,
Round and round the track?
Does Winston the bulldog let go of the ball,
When he finds and fetches it back?
If a Rottweiler looks at you with love,
Is he sizing up a snack?

Look, there's another dog I know,
Goes lightly on the ground.
Don't touch him for he's working,
And you mustn't make a sound.
Alert and wise, he is the eyes,
And helps his master round.

There's Nipper, the dog, on the record sleeve,
Where spins the singer's art.
How well he knows His Master's Voice,
And plays his little part.
In showing how canine pals can walk,
The highways of the heart.

So let us applaud the clumsy pawed,
Whose love is given free.
From mongrel pups to 'Crufty cups',
There's one thing that I see.
Whenever I'm down in the black-dog dumps,
You come and rescue me.

John Guy

Pinnacle of Devotion

Oh! my loving, agreeable friend,
Why as a dog are you disguised?
My life without you is deficient;
Not for once you have criticised.

There's none better than my life;
I adore it so as no one would do.
You desire nothing for yourself,
And you love me more than I do.

O my mate! I love you so much,
Though you aren't quite a wife.
You certainly make my life a joy,
And offer me a new lease of life.

You are faithful without doubt.
Your love for me is profound.
Divinity has granted your values;
I am blessed to have you around.

From you I have learnt a reality,
How to attain a contented mind.
One has to have selfless devotion,
For ecstasy of fulfilment to find.

Uma S Jaiswal

The Witch's Cat

The cat who rides the witch's broom,
himself, is blacker than the gloom.
His paws he stretch, clawed fingers five,
they grip the broom, he stay alive!
By blazing cauldron fur singed brown,
he tear in treads her old patched gown.
The sky at night, the moon she view,
he clings and dreams of rabbit stew.
Fuelled by goblins, understood, her
cauldron smoulders in the wood.
Older than time, perpetual flame, nobody
knows from whence it came!
Jack, woodman, as he passed along,
saw the smoke, to find it gone!
The puzzled fellow makes cat laugh,
he knows the witch's secret path.
As he tramps circles in a maze, it
disappears into a haze!
They watch him, tired, turn for home,
stung by nettles, cross, alone.
Over the treetops swiftly sped, and
with her broom, witch whack his head!
She cackles and her cat he hiss,
whilst glaring up he shake his fist!
Trout disappear from out his creel, the
cat enjoys a tasty meal.
Takes home no catch, but finds
instead, a pile of fish bones in his bed!

A E Doney

Dearest Billy . . .

The light of my life
My joy, my delight
That's Billy, my West Highland white

A ball of fluff
Just five weeks old
He came from Wales, so small to hold

Lots of puddles everywhere
Sleeping on Grandma's bed
Fresh chicken, baby rusks, certainly very well fed

Walkies daily from the flat
Up and down those stairs
Oh how much we all loved him - lots of work, but who cared

At the house he really loved it
Running from front to back
Nose under the gate barking madly - at every dog or cat

Up on the chair and the window sill
To watch the world go by
Never a quiet moment, even if we were to try

On the table, Bill's chocolate eclairs
(only Cadbury's would do)
In the cupboard his Cesar; rusks and sticks to chew

A basket full of squeaky toys
(All broken I might add)
He played with these after dinner - ran, growled and squeaked like mad

When bedtime came, it was up the stairs
For a rusk, two chews and a drink
Then on to 'Grandma's' bed - Billy, the best thing in my life I think

It was so hard seeing Bills get older
He'd been with us such a very long while
Such an adorable character - made just about everyone smile

But being a typical terrier
He'd not give up without a fight
In the end it had to be our decision - God only knows if it was right
Now there is only emptiness

Silence - but memories too
Nothing will ever replace Billy Dog - we wouldn't want it to

Billy made all of us happy,
Filled a special place in my heart
Cannot believe his little life is over - such sadness as we had to part

Bless you dearest Billy
You gave us only love
We shall never forget you - 'til we're in Heaven above.

Ann Englert

Cap, The Wonder Dog

To those who love the animals,
We believe that they can talk,
So I'd like to tell a story,
To convince all those who mock,

Once there was a farmer,
Who tended all his sheep,
Cap, his collie, helped him,
Intelligence beyond belief.

Sometimes when work was done,
They came in from ruthless weather,
Cap stayed close beside him
And they shared the peace together.

Much fun came when playing games,
With balls and other toys,
Cap in his friendly doggy way,
Could sing and dance with poise.

The bond that grew between those two,
Was a wonder to behold,
Each move, each look, each word they shared,
Made human love feel cold.

From animals we could learn a lot,
How strong their trust, their love,
Be kind to all God's creatures,
They are sent from Heaven above.

Margaret Findlay

Carla

We should have called her 'Gypsy'
For she loves to wander free
Exploring fields at 'walkies' time
Doing what come naturally

Well, she's only still a puppy
And she has a lot to learn
At the moment everything and everyone
She thinks is her concern

The times when she's corrected
Which is almost every day
She looks at you with soulful eyes
And anger melts away

Just like a woman! some have said
Knows how to use those eyes
Those two limpid pools of mischief
Can surely hypnotise

She came to us last Christmas
Which is now six months away
Don't know what we'd do without her
For we love her more each day.

Bell Ferris

This Is Me

Here I am, this is me,
My name is Tiff, from the Fletcher family,
Playing all day, it's so much fun,
Running around, 'til the day is done.

I'm a collie cross, and black and white,
I love to sleep, I could sleep all night,
Out for walks, three times a day,
I love my life, what else can I say?

I love my family, they are great,
But I don't like cats, that's what I hate,
I'm the luckiest dog, that's what I think,
I have meat to eat and water to drink.

Well that is all, that is me,
Look at my photo and you will see,
How cute I am, that is true,
My family think I'm lovely, what about you?

Melissa Fletcher

Charlie

Charlie, Charlie where are you?
Back of the chair or in the loo
You're scared of me I know you are
The man who's always in the car
With his dog who eats your dinner
No wonder poor Charlie's getting thinner
And who's the girl who plays with your hair
Yes it's that rascal and her name's Claire.

Roger Gerrard

Destiny

Dodger, what a brilliant name,
You have been through such a lot; it's really a shame,
That a dog like you could suffer all this time,
You are now on the road to recovery, hopefully feeling fine.

The future looks bright and a good home is what you need,
So keep your head held high and you will succeed.

Someone will care for and love you lots,
Dodger you can do it, you are the tops.
You have come through such a bad time,
Now all you need is a family like mine,
So good luck Dodger, all will be well,
What the future holds, no one can tell.

Jill K Gilbert

The Silent Purr

Tubbs you come to my bedroom
and jump upon my bed,
you tiptoe to my pillow,
your gentle paw touches my head.
A little miaow and as I pat your head,
a lovely purr says I'm going to love you
every day and every night.
You lie down and go to sleep
and dream happy dreams that are so sweet,
morning comes and I hear a miaow again,
then a purr from a cute sweet love.
Inside of you that I adore,
a love so sweet with so much care and trust,
and so loyal and true, that is the way I still think of you.
A special love cat in my heart
what a pity we had to part.
I miss you so, my own sweet love,
you may have died on Christmas Eve
but in my heart you will never leave.
Your body is in the garden,
you loved but your soul is here with me still, filled with love
and I expect that every night your spirit will jump up on my bed,
your little paw will touch my head
then you will lie on my bed with a silent purr
and a silent miaow, what a pity.
It's not real now but at least your spirit is still full of love.
My own dearest sweet love.

Gordon Forbes

Welcome To Kimi

Three and a half years I mourned you,
Only Max and me once again,
Tig you will always be with us,
But now it's with joy not with pain.

Then along came a little black bundle,
To help us start living once more,
Kimi you fitted in with us,
Your wet nose marks all over the door.

A little face waiting to greet you,
Then you lay flat out on the floor,
As we tickle your little pink tummy,
The look in your eyes saying more.

As Max settles down for the evening,
You nip him and won't let him rest,
We can see he suffers in silence,
But I bet he thinks 'you're a pest'.

In the morning the story is different,
As soon as I walk through the door,
I see you both play-fighting,
As you thump and bump on the floor.

Shirley Ann Chapman

Herbie

Oh I love my cat
It's he who rules the house
With his winning ways and looks.
In his presence I'm a mouse.
Oh I love that cat.

His fur's of burning gold
Shimmering in the sun.
His tail quivers when he runs
Ears erect full of fun
Kittenish and so bold.

Nearly tripping me too
He rubs against my legs
Purring loudly with content,
Winding round with a look that begs
'Stroke me, feed me do'.

His tail is seldom still,
It seems out of control.
When he's asleep it gives a twitch
He's heard our voice so droll -
Communication of will.

His appeal is rare.
His odd inconsistent habit
Of sleeping in different places,
A week here or there for a bit
On bed or floor or chair.

I love that cat of mine
His expressive yellow eyes,
White whiskers yet one or two of black.
A tiny white spot his chin underlies
Oh that dear feline.

Margaret Deverson

Stella

Our dog, Stella, loves to guard
And keep us safe from harm.
She takes her work straight to her heart,
Our garden is her farm.

We also like to feed the birds
And watch them as they eat.
But Stella chases flock as herd,
No meal for them complete.

She looks so pleased to see them go;
She wags her tail with joy,
Ignores us when we tell her 'No,
That's not in your employ'.

So, now another table feeds
The birds in our front garden;
So Stella guards the growing seeds
And wild birds dine with pardon.

Pearl M Burdock

God Loves The Goldfish

I am a fish and I swim in a round sea
It is a bowl and outside of it I can see
The god outside that looks after me,
Comes around with food at the setting of the sun.
He cleans the water every few days
When the water it gets dark,
And I call the bowl that holds me
And the water, Earth Ship and Ark.
They say I can't remember but I know it's not true,
Because I know when it's just about to get dark my food is due.
My god comes around to eat his dinner
And gives me a sprinkle so I can eat too.
What it is, he feeds me each and every day.
I know for sure because I heard him quite plainly say,
He pinches it up with finger and thumb,
And says, 'Little fishy, this is for you.
Fairy dust, just a sprinkle or two,
Because as you love me, I love you.'
How did I get my golden colour?
I know for in my heart he told me it's true.
He gave it to Grandad and Nanny because he loves them too.
Now they have gone to the fish bowl in the sky,
Where it's always warm and waters are clean and never run dry.
One day he promised, so I know it's true,
And this is why one day I would go to the fish bowl in the sky,
And if you're a good fish, you will go there too,
Because as he looks after me, he looks after you.

John Lye

The Softest Touch

Surely, nothing could be softer
than her muzzle
when she noses me to say,
I'm here.
It's morning; are you
in there?

I cannot help but smile each time
the gentle wishbone
of her mouth finds mine;
and no,
this warm, this slightly
breath-damp

Loving, laden with velour
just spiced with bristle
and a hint of crumb, is not
the softest touch;
nor I the only one who's
'in there'.

Hilary Lissenden

A Friend In Fur

There is a cat called Jake,
He lives at number 3
And when I'm going down his road
He likes to walk with me.

He chirrups as he walks
His tail is held up high,
He turns to see if I am following him,
Then it's time to say goodbye.

I talk to him like a friend,
I feel I am truly blessed,
He lives in Burlington Terrace
And I live in Romilly Road West.

Rachel E Joyce

Hedgehog

A little hedgehog hibernating for winter,
Snugly in a ball he is curled,
Sleeping tightly in his bed of leaves,
We won't see him till spring begins.

Waking up from his winter sleep,
He is hungry and thirsty,
With his water and milk, also cat food will eat,
Rolling out of his winter ball.

His spikes are shining and clean,
With his sparkling black eyes,
There with his long cute ears,
When people come along, home he runs.

When he shuffles along the leaves crackle and crunch,
There glows his black nose,
In spring his new spikes begin to grow,
There he walks along with his pink toes.

Courtney Paxton (6)

My Hero

He offers me his paw
To hold when I feel sad,
Then rests his head on my lap
And things don't seem so bad.

He's always full of fun
And loves to play with his toys;
To see him so content with life
Is one of my greatest joys.

He listens to my chatter,
Seeming to know what each word means;
But if I share any secrets,
He never spills the beans.

He delights in a long walk
At least once a day;
But am I leading him,
Or is it the other way?

When I receive good news,
He shares in my pleasure;
He's such a faithful companion,
My own canine treasure.

Annabelle Tipper

My Ideal Companion

I have a new male in my life
He is dark, caring and very handsome
When I wake up, his loving eyes
Already scrutinise me
Waiting to kiss gently my cheek
During the day, he follows me everywhere
He is always happy and grateful
For all the meals I prepare for him
He offers me everything he had
When we go out, he walks lovingly near me
Giving his fierce protection
I must confess, he is one bit possessive
But I like to feel loved and special!
I can honestly say I never had an argument
With my beautiful new mate
We are inseparable, always together
He is with no doubt, the ideal partner
But the only regret I have
Is that Jasper is just a soft dog!

Vicky Stubbs

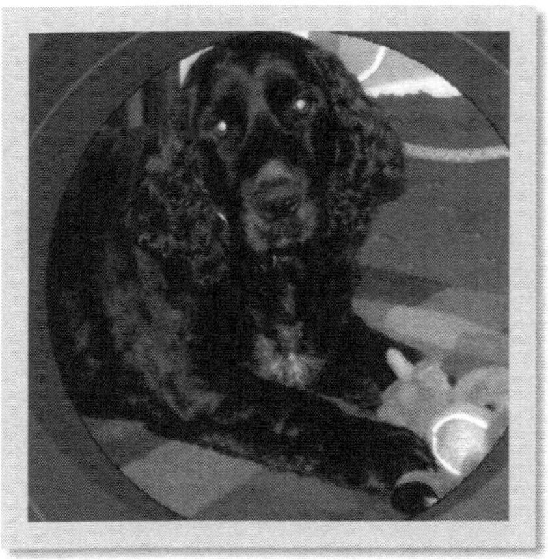

Ruby At Home

I'm new to the family
Ruby's the name,
And everything's lovely
I'm so glad I came.

There's a rabbit called Bobby
And a lurcher named Ted,
And everyone's lovely
I think I've just said.
A garden to play in, on long walks I go,
I'm over the moon, have I told you so?

I belong to the family
I'm everyone's pet,
I'm so happy to be here,
My tail's wagging yet.
But Sarah's my best friend,
Cos right from the start
This sweet little girl
Has stolen my heart.

Best friends forever, I know we will be
Oh I'm so glad to be here,
With my new family.

Jacqueline Claire Davies

Visited By An Angel

(In memory of Brogan)

I was visited by an angel
In the years that you were with me.
I knew at the time you were special,
But I couldn't quite clearly see,
That God sent you down here to guide me,
In ways that I needed the most.
He knew the best way to help me,
Was sending one of His heavenly host.

He thought out a way that was wonderful,
As a Westie, with silky, white fur.
He knew you would lead me out walking,
Taking me everywhere,
To show me the treasures of Nature,
So God's lessons I'd gradually learn,
His truth that would live in me always,
And the love, that I hoped I had earned.

You sat with me while I wrote poetry,
So many beautiful words.
You were here when I learned how to draw you,
While I eagerly listened and heard
God's message, in the song of the blackbird,
His voice through the sunshine and rain,
Felt His love in the joy that you brought me,
Now His peace, while from loss I'm in pain.

Lorna Lea

The Duck Pond

At our cottage by the sea
We found a pretty duck pond
As rural as can be.
All children love to feed the ducks
And ours are no exception.
So there we were, armed with bread
All set to try out luck.
Our feathered friends,
All shapes and sizes
Came to try our appetisers.
Of the large white geese however,
We weren't so fond.
They put us all to flight.
To see my family run round
That pond
Was such a funny sight.
Perhaps our aim to feed
The birds at night
Really wasn't quite so clever!

T Knight

Making The Farm A Nice Place To Live

The hare is happy and the snail is slow,
Cutting caterpillars, on leafy bows,
The ants are panting, ladybirds are dancing,
Birds are chirping and swans still swimming
And ducks are paddling, while geese keep haggling,
Fishes are fishing and bees keep buzzing,
Deer are charming and horses are winning,
Sheep chant baa and cows keep mooing,
Cats are lazy and dogs quite noisy,
Frogs are jumpy and toads quite lumpy,
Spiders are spinning a web so cunning,
Pigs are muddy and never stop grunting,
Hens are clucking and chicks are hatching.
All different, yet they all live together,
Making the farm a nice place to live.

Naomi Craster-Chambers

Sashi

Timid tiny ball of smoke
Eyes wide open and scared
Immediate adoration
Never to be compared

Wobbly, gangly, awkward gait
Bright eyes clear and aware
Wandering attention
Always a new dare

Torn curtains and broken pots
The one to blame is where?
Innocent expression
I was never there

Stunning, sleek and beautiful
Nose up to the sky
Confidently slinking
How gorgeous am I?

Sedate, serenely sleeping
Eyes shut, lost in dream
Purring with contentment
Whiskers full of cream

Struggling, older, slower
It's you that I adore
Needy for attention
Adventuress no more

Elderly, poorly, resting
Eyes implore release
Not wanting to continue
Now eternally at peace.

Karen Drake

Missing Monty

An empty lead, and an empty bed
An empty place where you laid your head
An empty space we cannot fill
An aching heart and tears that spill

Our lovely boy, our handsome lad
The daftest dog we ever had
But love and loyalty without measure
You were our joy. You were our treasure

Not nearly here for long enough
You were too good for Earthly stuff
A place in Heaven guaranteed
But all we're left with is an empty lead.

Heather Jefferies

The Artful Lodger

My name is Charlie Puddephat; some call me 'Mr P';
I live with Mrs Frobisher at number twenty-three.
We really get on famously and never disagree;
In fact, between us two, I think she really dotes on me.

Her culinary expertise just adds to her allure -
Her bouillabaisse the like of which I've never had before.
And, when she's extra pleased with me, she cooks my favourite dish:
A wonderful concoction of chicken, beef and fish.

While some might take offence, and resort to gripes and ranting,
She never even mentions my nocturnal gallivanting.
I even share her bed sometimes, which some may deem improper;
I actually fell out last week, and nearly came a cropper!

But before you draw conclusions, as I know it sounds uncouth,
Just allow me to enlighten you and hit you with the truth.
'Now that lodger's gone too far,' you cry, 'by treating her like that!'
Well, I'm not the blooming lodger - I'm the faithful pussycat!

Heather D Pickering

Precious Thoughts of You, Dear Danny

Tiny face and small brown eyes
Ears that flop from side to side
Constant bark that drove us mad
Yet still we miss you dear old Dan,

It seems like only yesterday
We used to love to watch you play
But when we had to leave you home
You'd always sulk or even moan.

The greatest memory of them all
Was when we both at last came home
You'd bound right up the drive to see
What treats or sweets we had for thee,

The slightest rattle of a sweet
You'd dash to sit beside our feet
Tail a-twirling round and round
Your paw then scraping on the ground.

You'd look at us so sad and blue
We had to then give in to you
Because we had no kids to love
You always meant the world to us.

Alas! it wasn't meant to last
Because one day we found you had
A cancerous lump upon your head
So to the vets you then were sped.

The news was bad as it could be
Cos cancer took a hold of thee
We had to have you put to sleep
Which broke our heart and made us weep.

Now dearest Dan, you'll always be
Loved and missed eternally . . .

Merilyn E A Gulley

My constant Friend

I couldn't bear to part with Ben;
my constant friend for many years.
He knows me well, and even when
I'm feeling down, he shares my tears.

He'll rest his head upon my knee
as if to say 'I understand'.
His soulful eyes look up at me.
He'll plant a kiss upon my hand.

But years pass by, one day we'll part.
I cannot even think of this.
For surely then he'll break my heart;
my constant friend, that I shall miss.

But in my head I hear him say
'I'll be there still, right by your side.
Don't cry for me when I go away
for in your heart's where I'll reside'.

I know he'll always be with me
his silent words I understand -
'You'll feel my head upon your knee
as I plant a kiss upon your hand'.

Pat Little

Copper Valentine Robinson (RIP)

(Long-haired Daschund Mach 2
[Mach 1 - Rufus Robinson - Short-haired Daschund])

You've helped us love more openly,
Through bad times helped us see,
Were born on Valentine's Day,
Passed over on Christmas Eve,
In my dreams I can see you,
Cradled in Nana's arms with Rufus too,
Now you have more family to love,
And loved by us here and up above,
You were the only boy in the pack,
Loved your tummy rubbed whilst on your back,
Were truly free at the seaside,
And truly at home by our fireside,
Your intelligence asked for the door,
When you played you used your paw,
Would jump over instead of going around,
Then pinned the 'rope-arm' to the ground,
Your tongue was out whilst panting,
To grab it was so tempting,
And we could without you minding,
Because your rope was more distracting,
Your lip went up when you smiled,
Your tissue fetish made you go wild,
You bossed your bed and bowl around,
Because they wouldn't answer to your sound,
You trusted us with your bone
Would listen intently on the phone
And even though you're gone too soon,
You will always still be part of our home,

And one last thing before I go,
You loved to play in the snow.

Lots of love from your family xxx.

Aron M Robinson

Dreaming

On the sofa there you lie
The best place in the house
All stretched out and in a dream
Oblivious to all around

Your legs start running
Faster and faster they go
What have you seen?
Is it a rabbit
Or is it a hare? Maybe a fox
Have you caught it? I'll not know

Now your tail starts wagging
And your nose is twitching
In your dreams, who have you met?
I'm just a mortal, I'll never know
Into your dreams, I cannot go.

Is it colour or black and white?
If you could talk
What would you tell
Of far away places
Where in dreams only you can go?

A knock at the door
You awake with a start
Back to reality
You give a bark

Do you remember
The dream that you had
A secret that only you will know
A doggie dream
That into, we mortals cannot go.

Patricia Plumpton-Edwards

Wildlife In The Garden

Moorhens nesting in the garden
Pond in the corner is their home
Always pecking in the shrubs there
Then round the lawn they love to roam

Nuthatch running up the trunk now
Of the weeping willow tree
Pecks away at seeds and peanuts
Does not even notice me

Blackbirds feasting on the apples
As they lay upon the ground
Singing in their safe environment
Grateful for the food they found

Dining on the old bird table
Many different birds I see
Chaffinch, goldfinch, blue tit, linnet
Eating there contentedly.

Yellowhammer, wren and bullfinch,
Blackcap, greenfinch, wagtail too
All these precious gifts of nature
In need of help from me and you

Beyond the garden in the green field
Many little rabbits play
Magpies, crows, wood pigeons too
On such a bright and sunny day

Angela Pearson

Fred

Do cockatiels live forever?
I know I am quite old,
From what I know, I'm twenty,
Well that's what I've been told.

Talking was my pastime,
I used to whistle and sing,
But as I became older,
Can't be bothered with anything.

I used to shred the wallpaper
And nibble the picture frame
But I cannot fly like I used to do,
Being good really is a shame.

You can't be good forever, can you?
So the only fun I get right now,
Is scattering seed and nipping fingers.
Shush, here comes a finger! Wow!

Mary Parker

Ben

(In loving memory of Harry Petty MBE and Ben, his golden labrador guide dog)

It really made my day
On my St Dunstan's stay
When I heard them say
'He's yours to keep today!'

I taught him how to beg,
When he should cock his leg
He won't sit still for long,
On the leash so strong.

Walkies dusk and dawn
Wakes me every morn.
Such a cheeky pup
'Now then Ben, what's up?'

He'll go anywhere for you
From here to Timbuktu,
Nowt's ever done or said
Just wants a pat on t' 'ed.

'Ben, slippers please,'
In his jowls with ease,
It simply never fails
Sits there, wags two tails!

Eyes that cannot see
A godsend just for me,
I'll never lose missen
'Good dog, Ben!'

Ian Tomlinson

Pets

What friends they make
They have such wonderful traits

Dog with a ball
A kitten trying to climb up a wall
What a great sight

They comfort you when you are hurting
They come and lick you better

They're playful and caring
They're willing and loving

Fluffy furry pets, oh how they are much more
They will have you rolling on the floor

They give you so much joy and pleasure
And it never matters the weather

Annamarie Cope

Smokey

(In memory of Smokey 'Bacon' Christie - June 2004-May 2007)

There's a new dog at home
And he's shaded black and white,
He runs and plays all through the day
And sleeps all through the night.

Not for him the pampered life
Of a pooch at home,
Over hill, under hill
'Cross the fields he likes to roam.

Amber eyes, you stare at me
Searching through my mind,
Other canines don't compare
You're so loving, and so kind.

Like an arrow out a bow
Streaking through the grass,
You can practically see
A cloud of dust where you have passed.

Hunting down your dinner
To a cheetah you compare,
Be it mighty stag or quiet doe
Or seagull, pigeon, rabbit, hare.

Of course, you rarely catch them
Yet you seem so satisfied
You seem to pant 'Oh well, hard luck
At least my best I've tried.'

But now your basket's lying bare
The straw has blown away
And you're not waiting in the yard
For me to come and play

You'll always be remembered
As months and years go by
There'll always be a marker
In the garden where you lie

Rhona Christie (13)

Pet Tiger

Not burning bright in nocturnal forests,
Only a cap-badge for a famous unit
Now no more - The Royal Hampshire Regiment,
Known to all the Army as 'The Tigers'
Because of their long stint in Hindustan.
They were there when that savage
Contretemps, the mutiny, erupted, exploded
Into a searing scorch of vicious violence,
Later they trudged through the Khyber
On the relentless march to Kabul
In the punishing Afghan war. Now
This tiger has been at last put down,
Laid to rest with many other emblems
Of lost regiments. His metallic roar
Silenced. Only his memory stays alive.
This tiger may not be a mincing pet
Of the tame, domesticated, cuddly kind
Or a Tiger Tim, talking out of old comics,
Rather a martial pet, living only
In the thoughts of old veterans, waiting
To fall out from their last parade,
Before death summons their last dismissal
And they can join their prancing tiger
In the limbo of lost memories.

P B Norris

The Talented Greyhound

My hound often raced on a Wednesday
But always trailed home in last
He said he felt bad for the rabbit
So let all the other dogs past

'Where're your balls? You must fight to the finish!'
'They went missing a while ago
I met a nice man one mid morning,
Next day I had nothing to show.'

Since the vets he'd lost all fighting spirit
For racing too chilled out and mellow
He was taken for walks now on Wednesdays
And encouraged to take up the cello

Course at first he began a bit smaller
Taking lessons on a violin
But his face was too long and unsuited
For resting the thing on his chin

Yet the cello he mastered quite quickly
His talent now opened some doors
High demand for a musical greyhound
Who plays Liszt on two padded front paws.

Won a place with the Symphony Orchestra
Off to Berlin we were now all set
Till the mutt went and foolishly ran off
With the poodle who played clarinet.

Stephen Hart

Thunder Storm

Oh Brother
I think I've upset Mother

Now you've upset our mum
Cos of what's in your tum

That brush she used to paint
No more it ain't

I told you not to chew it
But you had to go and do it

Anyway you said you wouldn't tell
So I said it was you as well

There was no need to tell
She knows you too well

I thought it would fill a hole
Better than the food in my bowl

I've told you not to bet
Not with her or the vet

You told me not to bet
The one to win would be the vet

Next time just lick 'n' dribble
Well OK just a little nibble

Oh! please for my tea
It's doggy food for me

As for tea - rice and chicken
That and a lot of bowl licking!

Clare Todd

Companion And Friend

TOBY was a little dog
His tail was very fluffy,
But when we took him for a walk
He came back really mucky.
So we rubbed and scrubbed him very hard
To make him nice and clean,
And then he gave a real good shake
Which almost made us scream!
Off he ran down the garden path
Jumping and playing with glee,
For he's so happy once again
Because he's clean and FREE!

Now we are pretty much like him
Our lives are marred and stained by sin.
An inherited trait through the human race
But the good news is... Christ died in our place.
To redeem us from the terrible fall
Sin's price was met *once* for *all*.
Jesus, God's Son, reconciled us to God
Paid the price with His own precious blood.
Sin's stains are cleansed and we can be FREE
When we come to the Cross of Calvary.

Christine Saunders

Lucky, The Amazing Hamster

Lucky was as cream as white chocolate,
He had a tail as long as the M6,
He slept a lot, nearly forever!

When he was awake, he ate chocolate and vegetables,
He had eyes as small as pinpricks; he was small and a bit skinny,
When I wasn't there he looked round with his sad eyes
Searching in hope as if I would never come back!

He loved to exercise,
When he was on his wheel it went 100mph,
When he went out of his cage he raced around
As if he was trying to win the marathon!

He loved to jump about, trying to get to the moon
And do lots of tricks, trying to show off,
He was loyal and obedient, like a little dog.

He annoyed me though,
Scratching and scraping like he was in prison,
It's as if he was saying, 'Let me out, let me out, please!'

He squeaked as if he was a mouse scared of the future,
Lucky brought me lots of luck
That's why he's my Lucky.

Sophie Humphries

Rejected Love

You do not listen when I speak of things,
You scold and curse me all the time.
You brandish power as if I had no value,
This painful, tortured, useless life of mine.

But things were different not so long ago,
You used to love me - or you said you did.
Have I so changed that now you hardly see me?
Am I so ugly that you wish you could be rid?

When I'm asleep I dream those times again,
When every day you loved me by your side.
I thought back then that this would last forever,
But my heart cries that now your love has died.

You seem so bitter, I wish that I could help you,
To realise my love remains as strong.
All you need do is give an indication,
Might you still care? Or am I being so wrong?

Your wife has gone, I know your world is darkened.
Because of this there is no room for me.
But time, they say, will work to heal the torment,
And then again, at last, we will be free.

Give me a chance to show how much I love you,
To gently smooth, the bitterness unlock,
My heart would fill with joy if only
You'd lift my lead and take me for a walk.

Harvey Lingwood

Party Animal

The cat is back
with a lithe imperious bounce
onto the window ledge, a bony spring
of urgency pawing at the glass.
The scrawny rasp of him savages food,
as he waves his split ear like a trophy,
frisks with his crusty nose.

Greasy as a punk, his quick tongue spikes
his matted fur, sandpapers his cuts,
possessing the sofa, he sleeps it off
like a drunk until his eyes are green olives,
his white pelt silken.
His purr is the throaty scrape of a jazz singer,
husky with the trespasses of the night.
He is a punk rocker defiant
with nose rings, a party animal
scorning our house rules,
a curling comma, rippling sensuously
between clauses.

Margaret Galvin

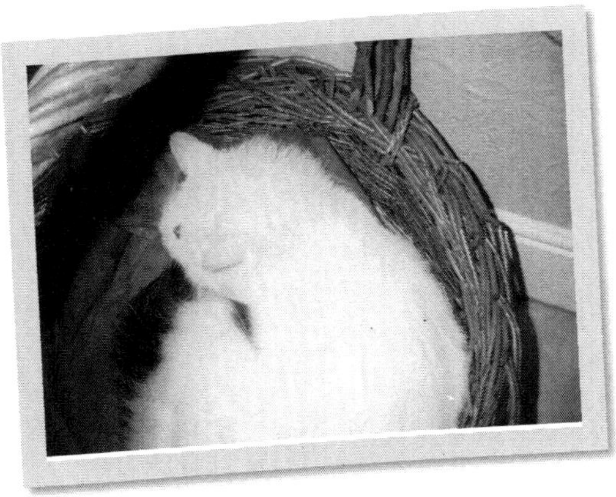

For Rita

I hate seeing dog poo on pavements
And horse poo in country lanes
And pigeon poo on my nice clean car -
Now that really is a pain!
Can't they go somewhere else
When they need a number two?
But hang on just a minute -
Where do cats go to poo?
They certainly don't poo on pavements
Or even in country lanes,
And thankfully not on my nice clean car -
That would drive me insane!
Perhaps they use our toilets
When we are out at work,
Or perhaps there's a smelly ditch somewhere
Where all the cat poos lurk.
They don't poo on your washing
Or pee against a post,
So I think we should thank our cats -
Let me make a toast!
To Rita - you are a pain sometimes
Especially when you snag my tights,
But I thank you most sincerely
For pooing out of sight!

Amanda Weeks

Rex

4 furry paws
A dripping wet nose
And 18 fingers
Or should I say toes?

2 pointy ears
1 very long nail,
Bright shining teeth
And a wagging tail!

A bark so sharp
But a touch so soft,
A smell that's horrendous
So much food he has scoffed!

So loyal, so friendly
As big as a lorry!
Touch his food
And you'll be sorry!

He's scared of everything
He's very complex,
I love him so much
He's my dog, Rex!

Rachel Robinson (10)

That cuckoo Is . . .

That cuckoo is a squatter
Anybody's nest will do
To lay their eggs in
As they look upon the view.

That cuckoo is a squatter
Any nest will do
They never bother about who builds them
Or if they are early or late.

That cuckoo is a squatter
Year after year
Yet for all their bad points
They are looked upon as dear.

Keith L Powell

Cat's Sonnet - or Cat's onnit!

She curls up on the sun-warmed window sill.
Content, she purrs her dreams, relives her day.
Paws tucked beneath her, tail curved round, until
A childish hand creeps near, intent on play,
And tweaks her tail. Annoyed she flicks it back.
Again, and yet again, her tail is jerked.
She makes it twitch, then leaves it hanging slack.
Her hackles rise, she's feeling somewhat irked.
The purring stops, her green eyes open wide.
She bides her time, she'll have a sweet revenge.
She's been disturbed, and feels she's justified.
With claws unsheathed, she strikes and is avenged.
A cry of pain comes from the little brat.
Her mother cries, 'Don't tease the dratted cat.'

M Peloe

In The Eye of The Beholder!

He is what is called tri-coloured, white, brown and black,
and he looks as if he's wearing a black saddle on his back.
His head and long soft ears are brown,
with a flash of white down to his nose,
his tail is black and brown with a white tip at the end,
which he holds in an elegant pose.

He has brown patches either side of his front legs
and both sides of his rear end,
and his under carriage is white, which down all four legs it extends.
Across his broad shoulders, his barrel chest
and up to his chin he is white,
with a coat short and shiny, to me he is a beautiful sight!

He looks as if he's got too much skin, for his body to be in,
that it collects together like a blanket underneath his chin.
His long soft brown ears they almost touch the floor,
which he often steps on, and over them he will fall!

The way he holds his tail, makes it look just like a flag,
and when he walks he wiggles his bottom side-to-side,
which makes his tail wag.
He has wrinkles around his front paws,
and baggy skin hanging from his hocks,
which makes it look as if he is wearing a pair
of *Nora Batty's old white socks!*

On his brow and around his droopy eyes wrinkles he has a lot,
and as he's got such short stubby legs, tall he certainly is not.
Which makes his body that is so long, almost touch the ground,
but to me he is my *Dudley dog*, and he is my perfect *Basset Hound!*

Sue Dancey

Corsilly My Dove

Innocent avian creature
with angelic flight in glamorous style.
Livid pecker of seeds in count,
patient and trusted friend
whose wing a silver light illumes.
Inlaid with cherubic emerald sheen;
and gleams of verdant gold.
Play o'er her burnished plumes
in pinions of brown speckles
emblazoned in contrast on the crest
reflecting with beauty and hue
to tantalising ray in unison.
Cooing with soft charming tirade of virtue
like a fauna with magical pipe.

Ogunbiyi Bamidele Julius

'I Love You So Very Much'

Already as a kitten
You had me smitten
Climbing all the way
Up to my neck as to say
'I love you so very much!'
How could I not be touched?

The very first night
You kept out of sight
A soft trembling furball
Nose pressed to my sole
You felt safe under the quilt
In the linen tent you had built

Caroline Skanne

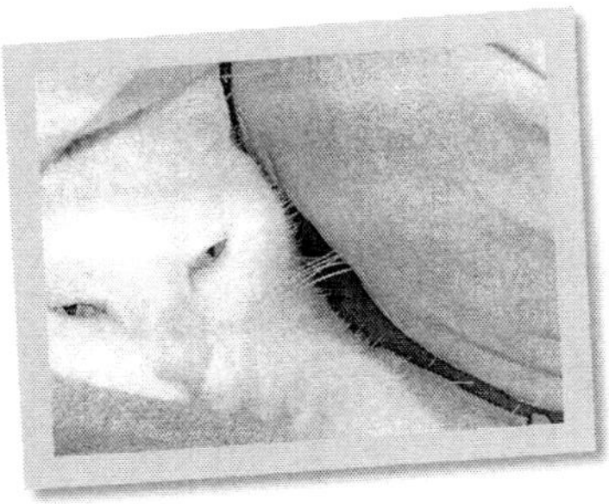

Kitty's In The Way

Looking up stairs mountain, heavy feeling in my groin getting worse.
I spy a black and white blob on the top step.
It displays an eye, brown flecks in emerald.
The eye narrows and another joins it.
I recognise contempt and am anxious.

Anxiety doesn't help. My need is urgent.
The guard cat starts to lick, preparing to present arms.
I climb slowly, two feet on each step, counting as I go.
The fluffy monster sits up straight and tall, far above my head.

'Mum!' I call. 'Need wee. Kitty's in the way!'
'Oh Joe,' Mum answers, 'he's only a cat, just walk past, he won't harm you.'
The rhythmic licking of my foe reaches his paws.
He bites at them. Bet he's sharpening them.

Two steps to go. Bathroom door in sight.
I jiggle around to stop an accident.
The slinky, graceful terrorist keeps me in his sights.
It makes me shiver. It makes me panic.
I make a run for it. Feline hackles raise,
Hissing and lunging with a razor-sharp paw.

Mum follows me up the stairs. 'OK Joe?'
I murmur my relief behind closed door.
Opening the bathroom door, I see the meaning of duplicity.
Mum is tickling Kitty under the chin. He rolls over and purrs like a kitten.
'He's only a cat, Joe, he just wants a bit of fuss, look.'

Kitty rubs at Mum's legs, shooting me a look of scorn.
She turns to go back down the steps.
Teeth bared, Kitty spits a final threat, then follows her to see what's for dinner.
He's always in the way is Kitty.

Linda Bond

Missing You

(In memory of Shannon, April 11th 2007)

I miss your head upon my lap,
I miss your grunts and groans.
I miss your bark, I miss your whine
Oh, how I miss your doggy moans.

I miss seeing you in the mornings.
I miss your presence in the night.
I miss your little tufts of hair.
I miss you so, it isn't right.

I miss your lovely greeting;
I miss you treading on my feet.
I miss these little things, so much
And I miss, watching you eat.

I miss seeing you in the garden.
I miss the way you'd run and play.
I miss you, when I'm home from work.
Oh, how I miss you every day.

Ann Potkins

Monty Versus The Bathmat

(A sonnet for my boy)

The remnants of the carcass removed,
The jumping, biting and barking subdued.
Monty walked away after having his fun
My poor bathmat was dead, Monty had won.

This wasn't the first mat that Monty destroyed,
It was the fifth such one I had deployed.
What about bathmats made him so annoyed,
I never did know so I consulted my Freud.

I left the door open by mistake when I left,
He soon went to work and left me bereft.
And off to the store I wearily walk,
With Monty in tow with eyes like a hawk.

As I placed the new mat he looked with a frown,
And I'm glad I'm not a bathmat when Monty's around.

Michael Frey

Sanctuary

You were born of Africa's magic
With a spirit, wild and free.
Now risen like the phoenix,
Capturing pride, and dignity.

Finally you've found sanctuary,
And again, can roar with pride.
No more will you be beaten,
Or from your captors hide.

At Villa Lorena shelter,
There's help given every way.
For animals that, have been mistreated,
Can safely live, for another day.

There you can bask in raindrops,
As they trickle down your mane.
Or slumber under a Columbian sky,
When the moon is on the wane.

History tells of mythical worlds,
And of many fables known.
But 'Jupiter' you're a king of gods,
And can make this place your own.

A true friendship not forgotten,
For beauty and her beast.
Which will remain for all time,
Till this world's cruelties cease.

Janice Thorogood

My Favourite Thing

I have the run of the whole bedsit
when my mistress is at home.
She likes to leave me playing
while she studies on her own.

I climb up on her desk to see
what she is writing there.
I nibble at her paperwork
or nuzzle in her hair.

I skitter across open books
that she is trying to read.
I spy and steal the chocolate
on which she likes to feed.

I skid along the floorboards.
I rifle through the bin.
It's a wonder she can concentrate.
I make an awful din.

Excitement builds as evening falls.
My mistress needs her supper
and I await with bated breath,
my favourite daily cuppa.

P G Horton

One Step At A Time

Help! I'm confused and I'm terrified. How did I get up here,
let alone in the middle of this slippery surface? It's glass by God!
It's solid glass. Well, I appear to have got halfway down.
I'm a brave boy - or on the other hand - I'm a brave girl.
Sammy? Cecilia? What does it matter what I am?
Oh God, dear God, please don't let me fall to my death.
The light's on the other side of this glass.

This funny lady has seen me. Come to think of it,
I think she's trying to help - sounds most encouraging.
I've now moved to the left of this bird lime splodge.
'Must be left wing,' remarked the lady. Now I lever myself down
an eighth of an inch at a time. Isn't she peculiar?
She's started singing, 'You can do it - *we* can help.'

Now she's wondering is I have any hearing and she's gone on to
'Here we go, here we *go*, here we go oh.' Down a bit more.
Perhaps I should be singing 'Rock of Ages'. Bit further.
Small - no - *great* step for the animal kingdom.
Good job I have some protection. Soon be on the pebble dashing.
More grippy grippy. Ooh *that* was nasty. Nearly on to the wooden bit.
She's just waved 'bye-bye' to me.

Oh boy - now I'm on the pebble dashing - wish it would stop raining,
but then that's why I'm *here*. I'm a brave girl. I've decided I'm female
after all and my name is Cecilia. Who said a woman couldn't do it?
'Bye-bye lady. I'm a brave snail.'

Pat Roffey

A Family Friend

Any animal, large or small has a place in life
I know of healing properties;
company for old people who are terminally ill,
brings smiling faces, like a sunflower of gold sparkle,
a way of communicating,
knows when a person is unwell,
brings a lonely person to life
like the seeing of a hummingbird's magnificent plumes.

Alan Hattersley

The Badgeman And The Birds

(January 2002 Edinburgh - Prince's Street Gardens)

A flurry of wings approach out of the cold, grey, misty
Edinburgh morning
Amongst them he stood barely five foot tall,
Dressed in a long coat and shirt,
Both covered in badges of every shape and colour
He makes quite a striking pose as he tends to his pigeons,
Badges rattling against one another
A faint sound in the city
Amidst a cacophony of much louder sounds
A sound that would have been lost
If I had not witnessed the Badgeman
Amongst feather and feet he stood throwing handfuls of grain
From an old travelling canvas bag
Beneath the blackened spires of the Scot Memorial
Akin to a burnt tier of a wedding cake
He feeds crumbs to sustain his friends the birds,
As he gazes up at historic castle amidst the heavy groan of traffic
He leaves them, walking back slowly through the gates
And then he's gone, dispersed into the busy throng
Of humanity beyond the gates
They stay behind to scavenge amongst waste bins
After he's gone to be ever hopeful for crumbs
And then too they are off, flying back into the grey mist
Of an Edinburgh day

Hilary Jean Clark

A Tale of Two Cats

All is silence, not a peep
Like cat voyeurs, we watch them sleep
Dreaming away the hours
Of prowlings amongst spring flowers

The butterflies you chase after
Your cuteness and our laughter
As curious little noses
Sneezed at the pollinated roses

Such innocence doth enchant
As a newborn nephew to his aunt
Tranquil, as a red sunset
Calm, as a storm unmet

As they sleepily awaken from their doze
A yawning purr and a lick of the nose
A stretch of claws, and how they mewed
A hungry demand, a cry for food

Oh cats, what a beautiful pair
As you lie upon the pillowed chair
What strange thoughts pass through your heads
As angels dance, and lovers wed.

Jeremy C W Bloomfield

Ginger By Name And Ginger To Look At . . .

In our garden one hot summer's day
A lonely little cat decided to stray.
Ginger by name and ginger to look at
He was furry and cuddly, cute and fat.
It was love at first sight so we fed him and fussed him
But the thought of no owners was a future too grim.
So we gave him a home with plenty of hugs
But one day we caught him drinking from mugs!
Ginger has one extraordinary wish
He'd love to catch my little goldfish.
He's an outdoor cat who's full of mischief
But often returns home full of grief.
With the neighbourhood cats he enjoys a good fight
And will proudly display a scratch, cut or bite!
One fight he lost when his bum got bit...
It was terribly sore and painful to sit.
A trip to the vets and an injection or two
He safely came home as good as new!
With food he's fussy about what he eats
Go Kat and titbits are his treats.
With one tooth missing he's got a hard life
Because he can't eat with a fork and a knife.
Ginger is special in more than one way
He curls up and sleeps on my bed all day.
I stroke him and cuddle him... Thank God he was found.
I'm telling you now - he's the *best* cat around!

Sophie Morris (9)

The Birds - My Pets

The birds in my garden are my pets
Always visiting whether sunny, snowy or wet,
So much about the birds I want to say
It makes me so happy, seeing them every day,
And when they splash about in the bird bath
They really do give me joy, make me laugh.

Blackbirds, robins, starlings - always lots of them
Dunnocks, blue tits, doves, finches and a wren,
Most of them will feed from the bird table
Eating raisins, bread, seed and peck an apple,
And the fat balls, into them they do tuck
Taking seed from the holders and peanuts.

In my garden the birds all love to visit
And in the shrubs, bushes and trees they sit,
Wintertime they eat the berries from the trees
Scratching on the ground for food amongst the leaves,
I always feed them, all the year round
Putting food on bird table and on the ground.

By putting food out for the birds in my garden
I know I am helping to make more of them,
Peeping out of the window behind the curtains
Watch them taking food to nest and back again,
When the young leave their nest, but are still babies
They all come to my garden to get food and seed.

On the garden seat I sit when sunny and nice
So as not to frighten them away I sit real quiet,
Always birds in my garden, never had a hedgehog
Did have a squirrel once and a frog,
The garden I have is not very big - only small
But the birds all love it - and I love them all.

Lindy Roberts

I'm A Clever Laughing Cat

Know how to be fed at night
With dry food, firstly polite,
Gently prod bare skin in sight,
No luck! Push nails in skin tight,
Wakens, feeds, too tired to fight,
I'm a clever laughing cat.

She thinks I should use my flap,
Growing fatter it's cat trap,
I'm built a well-rounded chap,
With paw tap flap, ignored, zap,
Up she jumps to open gap,
I'm a clever laughing cat.

If I dislike new menu,
Refuse to eat and poo-hoo,
'Eat up Pooch and don't pooh-pooh!'
She says, 'Change of food for you!'
Throw wobbly, it's back on cue,
I'm a clever laughing cat.

When friends call and do not kneel
To stroke me, they come to heel,
When I nudge, nudge them to feel
My soft coat their hearts I steal,
Paws in air, on back appeals,
I'm a clever laughing cat.

Have happy disposition,
No wish for expedition,
Found home on hunting mission,
Chase away competition,
Know my place, top position,
I'm a clever laughing cat.

Hilary Jill Robson

To Love And Be Loved

What a wonderful companion a cat can be
When you sit down he jumps up on your knee
He looks in your eyes with a love so sincere
His life is complete if you are near.

He is a very independent chap
And knows when not wanted on your lap
So if you don't love him anymore
He just walks out of your front door.

He'll find another with love to spare
With a warm fireside with him to share
So long as he knows you're his best friend
He'll be true to you right to the end.

Helen Johnson

Smiles For A While

There's a dear little cat who's asleep by my fire,
He belongs to my neighbour - just here on hire!
He looks for a hug, and he tells me a tale,
I ask him a question, he replies without fail!
He knows what I'm saying, he's really amusing,
But, sometimes he *can* be confusing!
If his folks have to travel he comes here to stay,
And brings his young sister - well that's OK.
They have fun and games as they run up the stairs,
And play hide-and-seek, around the big chairs.
In winter they sit side by side near the heat,
When it's sunny they're outside, asleep on the seat.
They may only be with me for a short while,
But the dear little souls, they do make me smile!

Jeannette Kelly

Mitzi

Mitzi was a tiny little pup,
A toy poodle you could fit in a cup,
The weeks went by and she grew and grew,
So clean, so white, so pretty and true,
Some men need a creature to use as a threat,
To meet danger when it comes rather than a pet,
Our little poodle was brave beyond belief,
People who need big macho dogs are often very weak,
Her little body would not deter a mugger or thief,
Mitzi was so clever she actually learned to speak.
'Hello Roy,' so clear, was never crisper,
I tried to get her to say 'Hello Mum',
She said this once or twice in a whisper,
We did not wish her to obtain public fame,
Football was her favourite game,
She was loved by people near and far,
This dear little dog you could not forget,
One lady offered to swap her for a brand new car,
Then came our saddest moment in the life of our pet,
At fifteen and a half she developed a growth,
We could not allow her to endure such pain,
Euthanasia followed, and I swear on oath,
We cried like babies knowing we would not see Mitzi again.

Roy Kimpton

My Emma

Today a cuckoo sang. A warm sun rose, enveloping
The blue sky which wrapped itself around me.
As gentle bluebells swung and the sweet smell of hawthorn
Soothed me, purple lilac hung
But I mourned. Today I lost my friend.

I ache for the years of total devotion.
I see her wagging tail, watch her trusting brown eyes,
I knew her need of me, as she bore her pain.
She trusted me with her wrinkled frown.
I grieve today. I am tearful.

She lay paralysed in my backyard
The vet helped her cope, with dignity.
I stroked her brow. She looked at me,
I did not let her down.
My dear black Labrador.

No more soggy paws, no more drooling jaws.
No more kisses in the early morning.
No insistent nudges at my arm. No greetings when
I come home stressed.
Just a dreadful emptiness.

She lies now under purple lilac.
I see the mound from my bedroom
Window. I smile, I know she knows I
Watch. Each dog's death is trauma.
But each one holds a special place.

Dorothea Carroll

Ode To Snooks

How sad we are that Snooks has gone,
We miss his friendly quack.
We miss his funny little ways,
And know he won't be back.

Dear Snooks was such a trusting duck,
And made a fox his friend.
He didn't seem to realise
What would happen in the end.

One day the fox felt peckish,
And Snooks looked such a treat.
I'm sure by now you've guessed it:
Poor Snooks, the fox did eat!

He ate him up so quickly
That, when Snooks was inside,
The fox got dreadful tummy ache
Gave one last groan, then died.

So when we came to bury Snooks,
We didn't need a box.
We dug a hole and placed him there
Inside his friend - the fox.

Colleen Simons

Trixie

Trixie is my brown-eyed terrier dog,
She pulls on her lead and makes me jog.
Trixie likes to beg on her back paws,
And she uses her nose to open up doors.
She's hyper and greedy,
And ever so speedy,
Her bark is ferocious and rare,
It makes people stop and stare.

She jumped in a lake,
Not knowing what was at stake.
I saw fear in her eyes and couldn't help make a fuss.
My aunty saved her, as she dragged her back to us.
She doesn't like motorbikes, fireworks or thunder,
I lift up my arm which she attempts to hide under.

Trixie loves the snow along with its taste!
Well, leaving it to melt wouldn't that be a waste?
I think if she could talk she would have to say,
'Stop global warming, keep Trixie and her snow happy today.'

The world revolves around her or so she thinks,
While rolling in the mud she truly sinks.
Doggie biscuits and chocolate drops,
When it comes to eating she never stops.
She may be silly and annoying at times,
But my love for her is more than could be expressed by rhymes.

Ellie Duffey (13)

A Fishy Tale

Our pet is a goldfish, we received him as a gift,
'Just watching him will calm you down and give your soul a lift',
That is what they told us when they left him here that day,
'If you don't want to keep it, throw the ruddy thing away'.

We kept this little goldfish, George is his given name,
To throw him down the toilet would be an awful shame.
We bought a bowl and fish food and sat and watched him swim,
We fed our goldfish twice a day because he was so slim.

Well George grew big and beautiful, his tail a sight to see,
But as for calming humans down... no this will never be,
Our fish is hyperactive, he dashes to and fro,
I never see him sleeping, he's always on the go.

He dashes round and round his bowl, he leaps, he dives, he blows,
And why he does this blowing thing only Georgie knows,
He fossicks in his gravel and moves his plants around,
I thought that fish were quiet things and never make a sound.

Our Georgie is a noisy fish, we hear him in the night,
I thought it was a mouse one time and had a dreadful fright,
Yes our pet is a goldfish, we received him as a gift,
He doesn't calm you down at all,
But makes you laugh and gives your soul a lift.

Doreen Mezzomo

Snoopy

My darling little Snoopy
I miss you oh so much
I loved you more than life itself
So much, you'll never know.
My life it seems so empty
Without your cheeky ways
Like how you tried to pinch
Chicken off Barbara's plate!
Oh Snoopy, why did you have to go?
Your time, it came so fast
But here deep within my heart
Your memory still lasts.
Now you're out of pain and hurt
And moved to start again,
And though I find it very hard
I must try to do the same.
I hope you've found a peaceful place
To rest your weary bones,
And I hope you're happy
In your brand new home.

Theresa Ann Sanderson

Love Shared

My love is a bundle of soft brown fur
With eyes of a deep brown hue
Whenever I go for a walk in the fields
A little brown body comes too.

I sit in the long grass and watch the birds
And the little brown body sits too
But as he is only a little chap
He doesn't have much of a view.

He looks at me with those big brown eyes
Willing me what to do
'Go back home to our nice warm house
And share a biscuit or two'.

Whatever I do he is by my side
So I know I'll never be blue
For that little brown body with big brown eyes
Keep saying, 'I love you too.'

B Williams

The Far Away Dogs

The Far Away Dogs in the dogs' home
Emptily howl in the night.
The treasures they've lost or are missing
I cannot imagine are slight.
Some have lost human companions
That they thought would always be kind
And others have body parts missing:
An ear or an eye or a mind.

The Far Away Dogs call together
With sorrow and shame in each note.
The sadness at losing a home hearth
And loving shows most in the coat.
It's furrowed, it's loose and it's staring,
Just like the face and the eyes.
As a madness is filtering deeper
See the soul of each dog vaporise.

If depression is often upon you
Take a Far Away Dog off the shelf.
I say this from grateful experience
Because I have seven myself!
The pain they've endured can't be measured
Yet the love that they give is unbounded.
My dogs are my world, my salvation,
And upon them my whole life is founded.

Lesley S Robinson

The Littlest Hobo

Went in my kitchen early one morning
I heard scratching and some gnawing

I saw something move at the corner of my eye
My heart was beating fast, I thought I was about to die

I look down, there was a mess on my kitchen floor
A small bundle of fluff was by the back door

It was a very young baby rabbit, a little stray
I gave it some food and made a bed out of hay

Three weeks later vet told us it was a female (a doe)
We are now her owners and we have called her Hobo

Brenda Wedge

Ruby

A puppy so small - one of thirteen
With a special twinkle in your eyes
They seemed to say please, please, please
Such a faithful friend, always willing
Never betraying or questioning
Each day you gave your all
To me you made life worth living

Amid my turmoil and grief
We faced life together
Life once shattered and torn
Every word you understood
Licked the streaming tears away
Brought joy and meaning
Love and hope

When you became ill
I knew
I would not let you suffer
The decision was hard
I had no alternative
Thinking of you always
Loving you still
Remembering forever
My Ruby, my girl, my world.

Marie Dutton-Creamer

Pansy Potter

Pansy Potter is the cat who drinks her milk through straws,
Who pirouettes in graceful rings around the ballroom floors;
The entrechat, the pas de deux, she's done them both with ease,
And other movements I can't name, which both enchant and please.

Her eyes are large and circular, and of a vivid green,
Her figure trim and beautiful, her coat a gloss black sheen.
She knows the waltz and foxtrot, she's swung from the trapeze,
And other movements I can't name, she's done as well as these!

She's walked with gay abandon on many a taut high wire,
Her dozen silver trophies are proof that I'm no liar!
In England, Wales, the Emerald Isle, from lands across the seas,
Those countless movements I can't name attract gigantic fees.

The triple half back somersaults from off the giant springboard,
Those feats of aerial daring, which make her fans applaud!
She always scorns a safety net, for thus she loves to tease,
And well she knows what I can't name she'll do as good as these.

She holds the world's most records in trampolining arts,
Gone round the board in doubles with the minimum of darts,
Done roller skating, aquaplaning, but still one hears the pleas
For other movements I can't name, yet quite as good as these!

It's true all that I've told you, hold no grave doubts of that,
There never was before or since so versatile a cat!
In isometrics, acrobatics, she's mastered them with ease,
And all the movements I can't name which both entrance and please.

Christopher Rothery

Where Is Jack?

Our dog, Jack, has gone missing, from where he was sat,
Jack's done a runner, along with the mat.
The mat he was sat on, the one by the fire,
The one that goes fluffy, in the spin dryer.
Where is our Jack, where has he gone?
I bet he's chased after next-door's ginger tom.
Or the other neighbour's cat, who looks like a rug
And sits on our fence, looking smarmy and smug.
I know what I'll do, call in the Army,
But when I phoned up, they said try salami.
Leave it outside in Jack's food bowl,
Then march up and down, as if on patrol.
So I said, okay, thanks for the advice,
But all that did was attract hordes of mice.
So I searched and I shouted, all the next day,
Was about to give up, as I suspected foul play,
Then I went into the garden and started to clap,
Because guess who was there, yes it was Jack,
With this wide doggy smile, looking no worse for wear,
Along with the mat, looking worn and threadbare.
I gave Jack a hug and said, 'Where did you go?'
And his eyes said to me, 'Wouldn't you like to know.'

Christopher Taylor

Meeting Richie

Lots of friendly attention as I walked in the door,
To let me know what I had in store,
This manic puppy jumping up to say 'hello',
Huge already but much more yet to grow,
At only twelve weeks though,
Learning can be painstakingly slow.

Suddenly he is rushing around everywhere,
So excited, without a care,
His attention span very small,
What next, the squeaky bone, cuddly toy or ball?

After a while he flops on the floor,
Falls asleep and begins to snore,
This manic puppy now peacefully lies,
Occasionally opening his eyes.

Dad comes in and tickles his tum,
Richie wakes again for more fun,
I call him but he thinks it is his mum,
And another excited performance is begun!

Later I try to go to the loo,
But Richie follows me too,
This now docile little pup looks up at me,
My heart melts as I stroke him happily.

Julie Marie Laura Shearing

Do Dogs Go To Heaven?

Well, I'd like to think they do!
And what makes us think, that souls
Are confined to me and you?
When I look at humans, and the evil that they do,
I'm inclined to think that animals
Are the superior of the two.
I'm sure they're sent to show us
What true love really means,
And will be there, to love and help us
In the land of future dreams.

Gladys Mary Gayler

Sweeta

(In memory of Sweeta)

Night was a longing,
A black hole waiting to be filled with your companionship,
Old enemies, the cold stars and their heartless master the moon,
Prevented me from seeing those deep twinkling eyes once,
They were the eyes that were my sun,
Waits merciless, meaningless,
How much did I endure?

Realisation - my nightly test was almost over,
I opened my eyes to the sunrise triumphantly,
Banishing darkness,
Early morning light allowed me to see your eyes,
Eyes that used to save me from the savage dark,
Suffering, pity, evil,
These words have no meaning.

I have found you again,
In my mind your eyes show your heart,
No longer a lost soul,
My loving dog, Sweeta!

Tarandeep Sandhar

The Great Escape

Spring cleaning
Opened the cage door
Oblivious of the budgie inside
Out it flew!
O look! Flying skywards

Following its wake
Hoping for a miracle
A miracle did not happen
Wishing for a miracle
To propel our budgie back - back to Earth
Back to its rightful home - downwards

'Come back!' I pleaded
'Do not go away
We love you'
A grown-up woman
Pleading for a bird's love
But it flew and it flew
A point of no return
Did not look back.

'My great escape!'
It seems to be saying,
'I am not coming back'
So it flew, higher and higher
Into the bright morning sky
Heavenwards
I stood there lost for words - helpless
For the children bad news - a loss

In the garden
By me stood the empty cage
Bits of food on the cage floor
Feathers, water bowl, climbing frames, toys
All that were left
Budgie is gone!
Gone to be with its friends
So I said goodbye and thanks for all the fun
The pretty blue, yellow and green bird
Is gone! Flown away. God bless.

Ellen Rollings

Monty

I picked him out from all those there
One black and white as I'd been told.
He was very small and young
He worshipped me and nestled in my hold.
When I got back home with him
He searched the room, saw ev'ry space;
We watched him first and then sat down.
We had a drink, he made a place
To sit on me and have a rest,
Then climbed up me, up to my face,
Down my back where was an arm
To give to him a resting place.

V Eldridge

Molly

Hearts melt like warm butter
with just one look from your soulful eyes.
When you want a treat or to be petted
you start with your down-trodden dog disguise.
We are always fooled by your mournful demeanour
though we've long since known your crafty ways.
You should win a doggie Oscar for your performance
and be a canine luvvie for the rest of your days!

You're energetic and playful and keep us all active
bring out your leash and drop it right at our feet.
Sit, shake a paw and even walk on your hind legs
all in the hopes of another tasty treat.
You love burying your bones in the garden
and going to the park to chase a stick or ball.
You are the smallest in the family by far
yet like a queen, you rule over us all!

Your black and white coat with a dash of dark brown
never looks sleek or well groomed and neat.
And the second you're bathed and brushed and in order
you get covered in mud from your head to your feet.
But you're our scruffy princess and we all love you dearly
you brighten up our days and make us all laugh.
When you come in all muddy looking sheepish and naughty
then look puzzled when we say that it's time for a bath!

Laura Martin

Yokko

More than 16 years ago,
we saw you for the very first time.
That first look towards *me*,
that look in your very sweet eyes, I will never forget.
You 'stole' my heart immediately.
So now the question to find a good name.
Maximiliaan (Max), that was the first *idea*,
but oh dear, that was a very long name to call you.
Then we thought of a really beautiful name,
and it suited so good with you.
And we got used to it very *soon*.
Bibel was so happy to see you again,
to be with you all the time, he almost jumped as high as the *moon*.
You both were still so small, just some months *old*.
Oh Yokko, I can still see you sitting near the fruit garden gate.
So full of rest, so sweet, so very special,
and I wanted to *hold*
you forever in my arms.
So many times you both 'flew' away, so very far till the end of the fields next door.
To stop when smelling a fresh *track*.
And when I called you both, you looked, okay,
but did not come immediately *back*.
You still had so much to do, so many more *traces*.
And when you finally came home, we only saw muddy *faces*.
More than 16 years we had the honour to have you with us,
to enjoy you, to love you, and we really did.
But then we had to let you go.
So many memories *together*,
so much has happened.
So much love you gave us all these years, all the time,
it could not have been *better*.
It was all so very special.
Once this difficult moment comes, you know,
but it always comes too early, too quick, too soon.
And most times unexpected.
This was the best we could do for you,
wished we could do all these years over again, once *more*.
Yokko, you touched our heart,
you were so very special,

there is only one like you.
And sometimes I still see you standing in the door.
Yokko, thank you for everything, thank you for all,
you are and stay my very sweetheart.

Florence Doornbos-Van Dijk

Kirsty 1982-'98

(Our family dog)

I miss the days,
With your little ways,
Such a great wee friend,
Ever loyal to the end,
You never did frown,
Or let me down,
You spoke with your eyes,
And told me no lies,
Still, you'll always be near,
As we know you're still here,
How nice it would be, as you sat on your mat,
Just to reach over, for one last pat,
If only you'd come back, for just one day,
Perhaps it would seem, you were never away.

Linda Wilson

Forward Press Information

We hope you have enjoyed reading this book - and that you will continue to enjoy it in the coming years.
If you like reading and writing poetry drop us a line, or give us a call, and we'll send you a free information pack.
Alternatively if you would like to order further copies of this book or any of our other titles, then please give us a call or log onto our website at www.forwardpress.co.uk

Forward Press Ltd. Information
Remus House
Coltsfoot Drive
Peterborough
PE2 9JX
(01733) 898101